Development Centre Studies

The Future of Rural Youth in Developing Countries

TAPPING THE POTENTIAL OF LOCAL VALUE CHAINS

This work is published under the responsibility of the Secretary-General of the OECD. The opinions expressed and arguments employed herein do not necessarily reflect the official views of the member countries of the OECD or its Development Centre.

This document, as well as any data and any map included herein, are without prejudice to the status of or sovereignty over any territory, to the delimitation of international frontiers and boundaries and to the name of any territory, city or area.

Please cite this publication as:
OECD (2018), *The Future of Rural Youth in Developing Countries: Tapping the Potential of Local Value Chains*, Development Centre Studies, OECD Publishing, Paris.
http://dx.doi.org/10.1787/9789264298521-en

ISBN 978-92-64-29851-4 (print)
ISBN 978-92-64-29852-1 (PDF)

Series: Development Centre Studies
ISSN 1563-4302 (print)
ISSN 1990-0295 (online)

The statistical data for Israel are supplied by and under the responsibility of the relevant Israeli authorities. The use of such data by the OECD is without prejudice to the status of the Golan Heights, East Jerusalem and Israeli settlements in the West Bank under the terms of international law.

Photo credits: Cover design by the OECD Development Centre.

Corrigenda to OECD publications may be found on line at: *www.oecd.org/about/publishing/corrigenda.htm*.
© OECD 2018

You can copy, download or print OECD content for your own use, and you can include excerpts from OECD publications, databases and multimedia products in your own documents, presentations, blogs, websites and teaching materials, provided that suitable acknowledgment of the source and copyright owner(s) is given. All requests for public or commercial use and translation rights should be submitted to *rights@oecd.org*. Requests for permission to photocopy portions of this material for public or commercial use shall be addressed directly to the Copyright Clearance Center (CCC) at *info@copyright.com* or the Centre francais d'exploitation du droit de copie (CFC) at *contact@cfcopies.com*.

Foreword

A large rural youth population and a growing domestic demand for diversified foods in many developing countries represent a unique opportunity to advance towards the three objectives of decent job creation for youth, food security and sustainable production, as spelled out in Agenda 2030. Yet, challenges to seizing this opportunity remain. Across the developing world, rural youth are turning their backs on small-scale agriculture. The gap between rural youth job aspirations and the reality of the labour market is widening. Under-development in rural areas makes it difficult to tap into the potential for increasing and changing domestic consumption needs and providing young people with decent jobs and living standards.

This study places rural youth at the centre of the analysis. It aims to sharpen our understanding of who are the rural youth; what is the nature of their job aspirations; which untapped opportunities exist for them; what are youth-sensitive approaches within agricultural value chains; and what can policy makers do to create an enabling environment for decent and attractive jobs for rural youth. A key message is that integrating rural youth into productive and environmentally sustainable agri-food activities rooted in inclusive domestic food systems may well be one of the few lasting solutions to the current rural youth employment challenge. For this to happen, actions need to be taken today.

The findings contribute to the work of the OECD Development Centre on building more cohesive societies and helping countries to identify emerging issues and find innovative solutions to address social challenges. The research was undertaken as part of the Youth Inclusion Project, co-funded by the European Union, to provide evidence for the policy dialogue on youth well-being in developing and emerging countries. It is based on the harmonisation and analysis of data from 24 developing countries in Africa, Asia, Europe and Latin America, as well as a review of development projects aimed at integrating youth into local agricultural value chains.

This work adds to the policy dialogue on rural youth employment in three important ways: First, it constitutes an unprecedented effort to understand the multiple profiles of rural youth and their job aspirations. Second, it takes stock of current approaches to integrating rural youth, especially disadvantaged youth, into local agricultural value chains. Finally, it proposes a broad policy vision to harness the potential of rural youth through vibrant, sustainable and inclusive domestic food systems anchored in local value chains. We hope that this study will stimulate discussion among development stakeholders to bring about environmentally sustainable food systems that contribute to food security and work for the large number of rural youth in developing countries.

Mario Pezzini

Director, OECD Development Centre
and Special Advisor to the OECD Secretary-General on Development

Acknowledgements

The Future of Rural Youth: Tapping the Potential of Local Value Chains in Developing Countries was prepared by the OECD Development Centre for the European Union-OECD Youth Inclusion Project under the overall guidance of Ji-Yeun Rim, Co-ordinator; Alexandre Kolev, Head of the Social Cohesion Unit; Naoko Ueda, Deputy Director; and Mario Pezzini, Director of the Development Centre, Organisation for Economic Co-operation and Development (OECD). The report was drafted by Alexandre Kolev (OECD); Maria Lee, Independent Expert; Ji-Yeun Rim (OECD); and Pablo Suarez Robles, Economist (OECD) in close collaboration with Bernd Seiffert, Local Institutions and Rural Livelihoods Officer (Food and Agriculture Organization of the United Nations [FAO]). Statistical and research assistance was provided by Toma Savitki, Policy Analyst (OECD).

The report benefited from field examples and technical inputs from international organisations, research institutes and non-governmental organisations with experience in mainstreaming youth in agricultural value chain projects and programmes. The contributions from the following individuals are gratefully acknowledged: Bernd Seiffert, Francesca Dalla Valle, Ileana Grandelis, Ajuaye Sigalla, Nomathemba Mhlanga, David Neven, Benjamin Doin, Oumar Syll, Cristina Rapone, Denis Herbel, and Boris Gandon from the FAO; Mattia Prayer Galletti, Elena Pietschmann, Ben Odoemena, Ibifuro Ibeakuzie, Lucia Di Troia, and Khadidja Doucoure from the International Fund for Agricultural Development (IFAD); Charlotte Goemans from the International Labour Organization (ILO) in Tanzania; Umadevi Swaminathan and Smita Bhatnagar from the Self Employed Women's Association (SEWA); Ken Lohento from the Technical Centre for Agricultural and Rural Cooperation ACP-EU (CTA); Christian Mersmann from the Global Donor Platform on Rural Development; Christophe Yvetot and Eduin Matta Castillo from the United Nations Industrial Development Organization (UNIDO); and Lucia Wegner from the Royal Tropical Institute (KIT).

The final report benefited from technical comments from Adrien Lorenceau, Arthur Minsat, Jan Rielaender and Vicente Ruiz, OECD Development Centre; Maria Rosa De Paolis, European Commission; Bernd Seiffert, FAO; and Mattia Prayer Galletti, IFAD and Christophe Yvetot and Eduin Matta Castillo, UNIDO.

The financial contribution of the European Union is gratefully acknowledged.

Table of contents

Abbreviations and acronyms 7

Executive summary 9

Assessment and recommendations 11

Chapter 1. Rural youth livelihood: A situation analysis 19

The global youth population will continue to grow until 2050, driven by Africa 19
Rural youth in developing countries are low educated and the majority work in poor-quality jobs. 22
The reality of the labour market does not live up to rural youth aspirations 27
Conclusion 41
References 42

Chapter 2. Approaches for youth inclusion along the agricultural value chain 45

Agricultural production provides an entry point for low-skilled rural youth to engage in the agri-food value chain 47
New job opportunities are emerging in agribusiness services 56
Integrating rural youth into agri-food processing activities will require skills training and youth ownership 61
Conclusion 66
References 68

Chapter 3. Towards decent work opportunities for rural youth 71

Promoting local value chains as an engine for the creation of decent youth jobs and food security . 73
Linking rural and urban development using a territorial approach 76
Adopting a comprehensive approach to rural development 78
Exploiting the opportunities in regional and international markets 81
Investing in agriculture and rural infrastructure 82
Greening and diversifying rural economies 84
Ensuring social and environmental safeguards 88
Raising the voices of rural youth in policy dialogue 89
Providing skills development and second-chance programmes for rural youth 91
References 95

Tables

Table 1.1. Structure of International Standard Classification of Occupations (ISCO) and broad occupation groups 26
Table 2.1. Total agricultural labour force 2016-20 46
Table 2.2. Criteria to select potential private-sector partners 48
Table 2.3. IFAD-supported PAFA's beneficiaries by value chain 51
Table 2.4. Enterprise performance, by revenue 62
Table 3.1. Training modalities in developing countries 92
Table 3.2. Constraints and incentives for private sector engagement in TVET programmes 93

Figures

Figure 1.1. Youth population by world region, in thousands 20
Figure 1.2. Distribution of youth by area of residence, % 21
Figure 1.3. Distribution of rural youth by highest level of education completed, % 23
Figure 1.4. Distribution of rural young workers by sector of activity, % 24
Figure 1.5. Distribution of rural young workers by employment status, % 25
Figure 1.6. Distribution of rural young workers by occupation, % 26
Figure 1.7. Share of satisfied rural young workers, using a raw and adjusted measure, % 27
Figure 1.8. Share of rural youth willing to change job and actively looking for another job, % 28
Figure 1.9. Distribution of rural young workers willing to change job, by reason and sector of activity, % ..29
Figure 1.10. Share of satisfied rural young workers by sector of activity, % 30
Figure 1.11. Share of satisfied rural young workers by employment status, % 32
Figure 1.12. Share of satisfied rural young workers by occupation, % 34
Figure 1.13. Career aspirations of rural students, by occupation, % 35
Figure 1.14. Youth career aspiration gaps among rural youth, by occupation, % 36
Figure 1.15. Rural young workers' skills mismatch using subjective and normative measures............38
Figure 1.16. Distribution of rural young workers by normative skills mismatch category and sector of activity, % 39
Figure 1.17. Distribution of rural young workers by subjective skills mismatch category and sector of activity, % 40
Figure 2.1. Number of agro-enterprises promoted, by value chain 63

Boxes

Box 2.1. Youth-owned inclusive businesses in the agricultural sector 60
Box 3.1. Selecting the right value chain: A chicken-and-egg problem 74
Box 3.2. Geographical indications for territorial development 80
Box 3.3. Transforming agriculture in Africa: Is CAADP the answer? 83
Box 3.4. Blue Economy and the potential for large-scale job creation 86
Box 3.5. Organic farming in Asia and the Pacific 87
Box 3.6. Developing entrepreneurial culture and skills: UNIDO's Entrepreneurship Curriculum Programme 94

Follow OECD Publications on:

 http://twitter.com/OECD_Pubs

 http://www.facebook.com/OECDPublications

 http://www.linkedin.com/groups/OECD-Publications-4645871

 http://www.youtube.com/oecdilibrary

 http://www.oecd.org/oecddirect/

Abbreviations and acronyms

ACP	African, Caribbean and Pacific Group of States
AfDB	African Development Bank
ASEAN	Association of Southeast Asian Nations
CAADP	Comprehensive Africa Agriculture Development Programme
CADA	Commodity Apex Development Associations
CDD	community-driven development
COMESA	Common Market for Eastern and Southern Africa
CTA	Technical Centre for Agricultural and Rural Cooperation
CUMA	co-operatives for sharing mechanisation tools
EAC	East African Community
EC	European Commission
EU	European Union
FAB	food and agriculture business
FAO	Food and Agriculture Organization
FDI	foreign direct investment
GDP	gross domestic product
GI	geographical indications
ICA	integrated country approach
ICT	information and communications technology
IDRC	International Development Research Centre
IFAD	International Fund for Agricultural Development
IFOAM	International Foundation for Organic Agriculture
ISCED	International Standard Classification of Education
ISCO	International Standard Classification of Occupations
ISIC	International Standard Industry Classification
JFFLS	Junior Farmer Field and Life Schools
NEPAD	New Partnership for Africa's Development
NGO	non-governmental organisation

ODA	official development assistance
OECD	Organisation for Economic Co-operation and Development
PAFA	Agricultural Value Chains Development Project
SACCO	local savings union co-operatives
SADC	Southern African Development Community
SEWA	Self Employed Women's Association
SIGI	Social Institutions and Gender Index
SME	small and medium enterprise
SWTS	School-to-Work Transition Survey
TVET	technical and vocational education and training
UNCTAD	United Nations Conference on Trade and Development
UNDP	United Nations Development Programme
UN DESA	United Nations Department of Economic and Social Affairs
UNSD	United Nations Statistics Division

Executive summary

Rural youth today constitute the majority of the youth population in many developing countries. Most of them are engaged in subsistence farming and struggle to find better-paying jobs to escape poverty. What is becoming increasingly clear is that rural youth are turning their backs on small-scale agriculture; they have high expectations, do not want to farm, and aspire to better jobs elsewhere. Yet, a growing local and regional demand for food in many parts of the developing world represents a unique untapped opportunity to advance towards the triple objectives of decent job creation for rural youth, food security, and sustainable production. The question for policy makers, therefore, is how to make rural youth the drivers of more productive and environmentally sustainable agri-food activities that respond to changing local and regional consumption needs and provide them with decent jobs aligned with their expectations.

The main objective of this study is to shed light on the potential of local value chains to create more, better and sustainable jobs for rural youth in developing countries. It prompts the following key questions: Who are the rural youth? What is their employment situation? What is the nature of their job aspirations? Which untapped opportunities exist for rural youth? What are the promising approaches to integrate rural youth into agricultural value chains? What can policy makers do to create an enabling environment for local value chain development that generates decent and attractive jobs for rural youth?

This study is based on the harmonisation and analysis of data from 24 School-to-Work Transition Surveys (SWTS) conducted by the International Labour Organization (ILO) between 2012 and 2015 among youth aged 15-29. It also reviewed development projects aimed at integrating rural youth into local value chains. This study adds to the global debate on rural youth employment in three important ways.

First, it presents a detailed portrait of rural youth in developing countries. The study shows that rural young people constitute a socially and spatially diverse group that often faces the double challenge of age-specific vulnerabilities and underdevelopment of rural areas. By and large, rural youth are low educated and operate in subsistence agriculture as self-employed workers or contributing family workers. Only a tiny proportion of rural youth hold jobs in high-skilled occupations although most of them aspire to these jobs. The majority are not truly satisfied with their employment situation and want to change jobs. Moreover, underqualification is a major issue for youth in rural areas and a problem that is even more pronounced in the agricultural sector.

Second, the study shows that agriculture and food processing represent an untapped reservoir of opportunities for rural youth. While local and regional demand for food is rising in many developing countries, the scope for developing and integrating rural youth into local value chains remains largely underexploited. Most rural youth engaged in agriculture are currently involved in production and very few are involved in downstream activities in the value chain. There are many reasons why investing in local value chain development in the agri-food sector could become an engine for decent job creation and food security. For one thing, local food processing is compatible with the relatively low level of skills possessed by rural youth, and is more likely to remain located in small towns and rural areas to ensure proximity to the production source. Additionally, it can create strong forward and backward linkages with other food and non-food system activities, paving the way for a virtuous cycle of territorial development.

Third, the study proposes a policy vision to harness the potential of rural youth through vibrant, sustainable and inclusive domestic food systems anchored in local value chains. Developing countries can make this happen, but decisions and actions need to be taken today. The following policy priorities have been identified to create the enabling environment:

- promoting local value chains as an engine for decent job creation and food security
- linking rural and urban development using a territorial approach
- adopting a comprehensive approach to rural development to develop regional advantages
- exploiting the opportunities in regional and international markets
- investing in agriculture and rural infrastructure
- greening and diversifying rural economies
- applying social and environmental safeguards
- raising the voices of rural youth in policy dialogue
- providing skills development and second-chance programmes for rural youth.

Assessment and recommendations

A large rural youth population and a growing domestic demand for diversified foods in many developing countries represent a unique opportunity to advance towards the three objectives of decent job creation for youth, food security, and sustainable production as spelled out in Agenda 2030. Yet, challenges to seizing this opportunity remain. Most developing countries still need to promote more productive and environmentally sustainable agri-food activities that can meet changing domestic consumption needs, create decent job opportunities for their large rural youth populations, and help close the gap between rural jobs and what youth aspire to. Developing countries can make this happen, but decisions and actions need to be taken today.

This study argues that countries that are able to promote agri-food and local value chain development through a youth lens are likely to reap significant benefits from their large rural youth population and the growing domestic demand for more sophisticated and quality food products. However, missing this opportunity will likely lead to increased frustration among rural youth, with the chilling consequences that unmet aspirations of numerous youth can generate, including social unrest and rural exodus.

Making rural life and rural jobs more attractive to youth will require tapping into the potential of agricultural value chains, and understanding the opportunities and challenges of food and agriculture systems in developing countries. The study therefore places rural youth at the centre of the analysis and asks: Who are the rural youth? What is the nature of their job aspirations? Which untapped opportunities exist for rural youth? What are the promising approaches to integrate rural youth into agricultural value chains? What can policy makers do to create an enabling environment for local value chain development that can generate decent and attractive jobs for rural youth?

An important objective of this study is to present a comprehensive policy vision that can help developing countries transform their rural economies in ways that preserve the planet and work for the majority of rural youth. The report starts by presenting a portrait of rural youth; looking at their numbers, employment situation, skills and career aspirations; and comparing them with their urban peers (Chapter 1). It examines current experiences in developing countries to integrate youth, especially disadvantaged youth, into the production, transformation and diversification of the agri-food sector and related services. It then identifies success factors to increase participation of youth in agricultural and local value chains (Chapter 2). The report concludes with policy recommendations to build vibrant, sustainable and inclusive food systems that can benefit youth (Chapter 3).

Rural young people face the double challenge of age-specific vulnerabilities and underdevelopment of rural areas

Rural youth constitute the largest proportion of the youth population in many developing countries and their number is expected to increase in the least developed countries, mainly due to the combination of high fertility rates and decreasing mortality rates. The countries with the highest proportion of rural youth can be found in the Horn of Africa, the Sahel and Southern Asia. Rural young people are a socially and spatially diverse group, and several factors influence their employment outcomes, including their level of education and skills, gender, location, social norms, role models, social networks, household poverty level and access to assets such as land, finance and knowledge.

Rural young people face age-specific vulnerabilities in addition to the challenge of living in underdeveloped areas. They suffer from low opportunities to receive quality education and vocational training, limited access to land and finance, and a lack of voice in decision-making. Data on school-to-work transition from 24 developing countries[1] show that one in five rural youth never attended school and almost half of them have at best completed primary education. Rural youth who complete vocational education (10.7%) or tertiary education (10.5%) are only a minority. By contrast, a large majority of urban youth go beyond primary school to complete higher levels of education (33.3% in general secondary education, 11.5% in vocational education, and 18.1% in tertiary education). Rural youth in sub-Saharan African countries and in low-income economies have the lowest educational attainment levels.

Agriculture is an unattractive livelihood option for rural youth

Agriculture is the main provider of jobs for rural youth, but the pay, the stability of employment and the quality of jobs are low. Agriculture accounts on average for 37% of rural youth employment, but it reaches very high levels in low-income economies such as Liberia (63%), Malawi (64%), Uganda (71%) and Madagascar (79%). Rural youth are predominantly in vulnerable employment. Self-employment and contributing to family work, which are considered vulnerable employment, together constitute 49% of rural youth employment on average and represent by far the dominant employment statuses in the least developed countries. Few rural youth (13%) hold high-skilled occupations (high-skilled white-collar jobs) and the majority (72%) are in medium-skilled occupations, which range from clerical support (non-manual labour) to agriculture and factory workers (manual labour).

By and large, young people do not want to farm and there is a large gap between rural youth career aspirations and the reality of the labour market. Data from the School-to-Work Transition Surveys (SWTS) of the 24 developing countries studied show that the majority of youth are not truly satisfied with their employment situation and want to change jobs, even more so in rural settings and in the agricultural sector. For all sectors, the main reason for wanting to change jobs is low pay, followed by the temporary nature of employment and the poor working conditions. In agriculture, rural youth willing to change jobs are more concerned with improving their working conditions than those in other sectors.

The gap between rural youth job aspirations and the reality of the labour market is wide

Rural youth also have high job aspirations. The vast majority (76%) of rural youth aspire to work in high-skilled occupations, but in reality few (13%) are in such occupations. Urban youth also aspire to high-skilled occupations (82.4%), but by comparison with rural youth, more of them get these positions (21.3%). Additionally, less than half (39%) of rural young workers have the level of education required for their current occupation. Skills mismatch is therefore a major issue for youth in rural areas – a mismatch that is mainly attributable to underqualification (43%). This issue is particularly more pronounced in the agricultural sector than in other sectors. Skills mismatch is less severe in urban areas.

There are untapped opportunities in the agri-food sector to create decent jobs for rural youth

Domestic demand for diversified foods is rising in many developing countries and agri-food value chain development presents a real opportunity to support local enterprises and improve market structures and business environments that can result in more entrepreneurs as well as wage jobs. Building capabilities of rural youth to integrate into agri-food industries (production, processing, preservation and other handling processes as well as packaging and marketing) remains largely underexploited. In West Africa, a study estimates that the food economy, which includes producing food and retailing food to consumers, already accounts for 64% of working youth, but the majority of them are in the low end of the value chain, mostly in agricultural production, whereas off-farm jobs downstream in the value chain, e.g. in processing and services, constitute a minor share.

Agri-food industries are labour-intensive and can create jobs in rural areas, as well as ensure food security in these regions. Food processing is particularly relevant for job creation in rural areas because agro-industries are more likely than other sectors to be located in small towns and rural areas to ensure proximity to the production source. In addition, food processing creates strong forward and backward linkages with other food and non-food system activities, implying potentially large wage employment effects in local economies. Furthermore, the agri-food processing sector tends to employ low-skilled labour, providing wage job opportunities for the current large number of low-educated rural youth and rural women in developing countries.

Youth-sensitive approaches can help youth inclusion along the agri-food value chain

A careful review of projects aimed at integrating youth, especially disadvantaged rural youth, through local value chain development shows that the majority of projects were involved in the production phase, with few found downstream in the value chain. This shows that mechanisation of agriculture can indeed promote the creation of attractive jobs for youth in rural areas, including in non-farming activities, such as tractor driving or mechanical repair of agricultural machinery. Other jobs in service provision using information and communications technologies (ICTs) and agro-processing are also starting to emerge. Applying a youth employment lens to agricultural value chain development means to purposefully set youth inclusion and youth employment as an objective. The following summarise some common success factors to ensure youth-sensitive value chain projects:

- Rural youth profiling: Understanding the nature and conditions under which the different youth groups are engaged or excluded, and the generational and power dynamics along the value chains, will help identify the bottlenecks to be addressed when designing a youth-sensitive agricultural value chain project. This means profiling the rural youth population by age groups (e.g. 15-17 year-olds will have different challenges, aspirations and skill sets than 18-35 year-olds), ethnicity (e.g. indigenous groups), disability, gender, education and skills level, social capital, access to land and finance, prevailing social norms, etc.

- Selection of high-potential value chain: Young people should be involved in identifying a list of potential activities in their village and region which they consider themselves capable of doing and which at the same time represent potential growth sectors.

- Mentorship and role models: Young people need role models to look up to and follow. Agriculture is associated with hardship and poverty and is considered an unattractive option for young people. Local leaders and other youth farmers can help change the mentality of rural youth through mentoring and coaching. Mentoring can happen through incubator approaches, where young farmers learn how to operate a business or through regular meetings and interactions.

- Peer-to-peer learning: The most effective way to convince young people is through other young people. Peer-to-peer learning has proven effective when providing agricultural extension services, for example. Recently, an increasing number of young people with higher education are starting agri-food businesses. They serve as models for other young people, and play an important role in creating and investing in small industries in rural areas, building networks, and generating employment.

- Awareness campaigns: The potential of agriculture and value addition is largely underestimated. Young people in rural areas need to be informed about the different activities possible along the value chain if their minds are to be changed about agriculture and related jobs. Campaigns should include information about market requirements, product standards, innovative tools and new production methods.

- Basic skills training: The majority of rural youth are early school dropouts and have low skills. Programmes that provide apprenticeship and on-the-job training opportunities for rural youth can increase their employability. Vocational training programmes must also consider teaching soft skills in addition to basic literacy and numeracy skills. Improving entrepreneurship skills, for example, entails training not only in business management but also in negotiation, leadership and team building.

- Physical proximity: Activities must take place close to young people's homes. This is especially relevant for young women who cannot travel far to attend training or take up a job.

- Financial or in-kind capital: Access to land for young people is difficult, and rural areas are underserved by formal financial institutions. Furthermore, financial services are not adapted to the specific needs and constraints of youth (e.g. lack of collateral and financial resources). For youth below the age of 18, it is even more difficult and often impossible to access financial support. Activities aimed at helping young people engage in agriculture will need to support access to land, seed capital and/or materials to get started. Access to land, in particular, will be a critical decision factor for the youth, whether to engage in farm or non-farm activities and/or to migrate.

- Social capital: Agriculture is foremost about know-how and linkages with actors along the value chain. Young people tend to lack both. Joining farmers' organisations or co-operatives will help gain trust and solidarity, as well as make access to quality inputs, services, finance and markets easier. Agricultural co-operatives have proven to be an effective mechanism for engaging young people in agriculture and increasing social capital and employment opportunities through on-farm and off-farm activities. However, hierarchical structures, high membership fees, access to land and other co-operative membership conditions which young people cannot meet exclude them from benefiting from these organised structures.

- Modern agriculture and rural areas: For agriculture to become attractive to young people it has to be less labour-intensive and use modern technology. This can be in the form of mechanisation, such as tractors or improved post-harvest management techniques, as well as through the use of ICTs, to ensure that they have better access to information, services and markets. Basic infrastructure (electricity, water, road, Internet) will need to be improved for young people if rural livelihoods are to become more attractive to them. Some ICTs allow young entrepreneurs to start new businesses in service provision along the agricultural value chains.

The potential of rural youth can be harnessed through vibrant, sustainable and inclusive domestic food systems anchored in local value chains

Countries must think strategically about how to position themselves with respect to market competition while ensuring that business models are inclusive of small-scale producers and local businesses operated by rural youth. In particular, promoting jobs downstream in the agricultural value chain requires higher-skilled young people on the supply side, while at the same time boosting the demand side through a mix of market-based policies and identification of specific sectors or industries with comparative advantages. Policies can support rural youth employment demand along the agricultural value chain if they provide the right enabling environment.

Value chain development initiatives seldom apply an employment lens, and even less often apply a youth employment lens. Their objectives are usually about increasing revenues and export volumes, meeting consumer needs, and improving efficiencies along supply chains. Governments can play an important role in enacting legislation and implementing regulations, incentives, support schemes and standards to identify and promote agricultural value chains that create farm and non-farm employment for youth. Policies must be designed taking into account the constraints and priorities of rural young men and women. The following policy areas have been prioritised:

1. **Promote local value chains as an engine for decent job creation and food security.** The growing domestic demand in agri-food products both in quantity and diversity is largely underexploited. Promoting local value chain development is not only necessary for youth inclusion but also for ensuring food security in the context of rapid urbanisation, increasing dependence on food and feed imports, and growing domestic demands. Policy actions are needed at the macro, meso and micro levels. At the macro level, there are regulatory frameworks, national development strategies and trade policies that will support or hinder certain value chains. At the meso level, there are industry standards and businesses that will determine the channels and efficiencies of the value chains. At the micro level, there are small-scale producers and young people who need capacity building, skills and equipment upgrades, and access to capital in order to integrate into the value chain as self-employed workers or wage workers. Using a value chain approach to development means working on all three levels at the same time and

ensuring coherence and balance between local development potential and national regulatory and trade frameworks.

2. **Link rural and urban development using a territorial approach.** Focusing resources and investments in the development of secondary towns would offer new markets to small farmers and processors while creating job opportunities, e.g. in the service and retail sector. In Africa, the growth of towns and intermediary cities has strengthened the reciprocal linkages between rural and urban development. Investments should go into strengthening rural-urban linkages and prioritising transport and marketing infrastructure to improve market access and value addition, reduce post-harvest losses, and expand input markets and support services in rural areas.

3. **Adopt a comprehensive approach to rural development to develop regional advantages.** Growth in productive sector wage employment will need to be stimulated to address youth employment challenges. The regions that have successfully increased demand for labour are those where the proportion of productive sector wage earners in total employment has been rising. Unless demand for labour expands, it is difficult to design and implement programmes to increase the inclusion of disadvantaged youth. Investments to promote growth sectors in rural areas in line with the comparative advantage of the territory (e.g. geographical indications) and to support access to markets can contribute to the creation of farm and off-farm wage employment.

4. **Exploit the opportunities in regional and international markets.** Despite the large share of agriculture in gross domestic product (GDP), many developing countries are increasingly dependent on imports. About 85% of global value chain trade in value added takes place in and around three regional hubs: East Asia, Europe and North Africa. Global agro-industrial exports have diversified significantly since the late 1990s towards processed and high-value horticultural products. In Africa, the diversity of agriculture and climate provides major opportunities for regional trade. However, currently only about 10% of agricultural trade is from within the region. Border trade continues to incur high transaction costs from administrative red tape and bribes. Simplification, greater transparency and harmonisation of procedures are required.

5. **Invest in agriculture and rural infrastructure.** The Food and Agriculture Organization (FAO) estimates that net investments of more than USD 80 billion a year are needed if food production is to keep pace with rising demand as incomes grow and the world population will exceed 9 billion in 2050. The United Nations Conference on Trade and Development's (UNCTAD's) survey of investment promotion agencies in developing and transition economies consider the best targets in their countries to be in the agricultural and agribusiness industry, along with the transport and telecommunications, hotel and restaurant, construction, and extractive industries. Moreover, there is an increase in intra African flows, an encouraging trend, as it may help reduce Africa's dependence on extra-continental foreign direct investment (FDI) to stimulate its economies. Greater efforts from governments are needed to meet the Comprehensive Africa Agriculture Development Programme's (CAADP's) goal of investing 10% of national budgets in agriculture and to attract FDI in ways which complement and promote, and do not "crowd out", domestic agri food system actors. Finally, for agriculture to really become a competitive industry in developing countries, more

investment in agricultural research is needed to improve technology use in this sector while ensuring environmental and social sustainability.

6. **Green and diversify rural economies.** Rural populations often depend directly on the environment and natural resources for their livelihoods, such as in agriculture, forestry, fisheries, mining and tourism. However, the ecosystems on which they rely are increasingly threatened by excessive and unsustainable exploitation. Greening the rural economy will be key to boosting resource and labour productivity, reducing poverty, increasing income opportunities and improving youth well-being in rural areas. The modernisation of agriculture and the expansion of ICTs, products and services around renewable energies (e.g. solar, biogas) therefore hold employment opportunities for youth, especially rural youth. The job creation potential through the production and supply of clean energy systems is significant in rural economies, as the majority of the 1.5 billion people who do not have access to electricity live in rural areas. Other non-farm opportunities, such as ecotourism, have significant economic and employment potential for rural areas.

7. **Apply social and environmental safeguards.** Since the early 2000s, large-scale industrial agriculture in some developing countries in response to the global increased demand for food, fibre and fuel has led to deforestation and use of chemicals to increase productivity at the detriment of biodiversity and the environment. Rising concerns over these issues and denunciations have forced multinational agri-food companies to ensure that they themselves and actors along their supply chain are applying responsible and sustainable methods of production and manufacturing. Multinational companies play an important role not only in ensuring inclusive value chains but also in training and hiring young people. Several guidelines and principles exist to ensure that responsible business is conducted, and these should be strictly applied and monitored.

8. **Raise the voices of rural youth in policy dialogue.** Participation of young women and men in the design and implementation of policies is an important part of ensuring that their needs and aspirations are taken into account. Little information is available on the level of participation of youth in policy processes related to agriculture and rural development, especially at national level. There are different levels of participation: providing information, consulting decision-maker initiated, consulting, youth-initiated, shared decision-making or co-management, and autonomy. Rural youth need to acquire certain skills, e.g. communication and leadership, in order to participate actively in policy dialogues. These skills are also important within youth groups/organisations to build trust and a common voice and when partnering with other organisations.

9. **Provide skill development and second-chance programmes for rural youth.** Despite the potential for new jobs in agri-food value chains and non-farm activities in rural areas, the majority of rural youth in developing countries are low educated and low skilled. Skills mismatch, mostly related to underqualification, hinders any attempt at moving up the value chain or getting better jobs. At the same time, private sector employers, including small and medium enterprises (SMEs) struggle to find qualified candidates to fill posts, even in promising sectors where labour demand is high. Traditional technical and vocational education and training (TVET) programmes either fail to reach out-of-school and low-educated youth or do not provide training on subjects that are

relevant for the labour market. Various training modalities and a wealth of information exist on what works and what does not in TVET. Collaboration with the private sector to train a young labour force should be further explored. For example, more incentive schemes for SMEs to invest in youth skills development should be developed.

Notes

[1] Armenia, Bangladesh, Benin, Cambodia, Republic of the Congo, Dominican Republic, Egypt, Former Yugoslav Republic of Macedonia (FYROM), Jamaica, Jordan, Kyrgyzstan, Liberia, Madagascar, Malawi, Moldova, Nepal, Peru, Serbia, Tanzania, Tunisia, Uganda, Ukraine, West Bank and Gaza, and Zambia.

Chapter 1. Rural youth livelihood: A situation analysis

One in six persons in the world today is a youth. The majority of young people in developing countries reside in rural settings and most of them want to change their current employment situation and do not want to farm. Career aspirations of rural youth are as high as youth in urban areas but the labour market offers few decent wage employment opportunities. This chapter explores data from 24 developing countries to look in detail at the education and employment status of rural young people, their career aspirations and the gap with the reality of the labour market. It identifies factors that drive job satisfaction among rural youth.

The global youth population will continue to grow until 2050, driven by Africa

The global youth population today is at its highest ever. The number of youth between the ages of 15 and 24 reached 1.2 billion in 2015 (UNDESA, 2017). This means that one in six persons in the world is a youth. The highest proportion today lives in Africa and Asia (Figure 1.1). While the youth population is expected to decrease in Asia and Europe, it will most likely increase in Africa, at least until 2050, when it is expected to exceed 400 million, according to population projections. By 2030, the number of youth is projected to increase by 42% in Africa. In Asia, the number is projected to decline from 718 million to 711 million, but remaining the region with the highest number of youth. The decrease in Asia is due to lower fertility in the context of urbanisation and rising life expectancy, whereas in sub-Saharan Africa the fertility rates are expected to remain high, with life expectancy increasing slowly (UNDESA, 2015). Sub-Saharan Africa has the youngest (median age of 18.3 years) and the world's fastest growing population (2.8% per year since mid-2000s (World Bank/IFAD, 2017). Global youth population will reach 1.3 billion by 2030.

Figure 1.1. Youth population by world region, in thousands

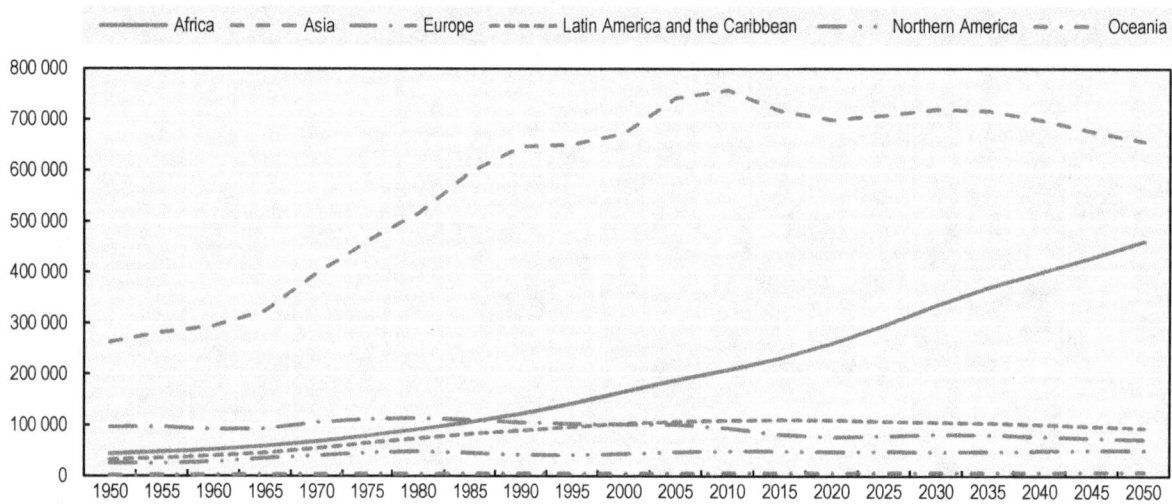

1. Youth are aged 15-24.
2. Population projections for the period 2015-50 are based on the medium fertility variant.
Source: UNDESA (2017), *World Population Prospects: The 2017 Revision*, custom data acquired via website.

These young people are entering the world of work with high expectations. It is expected that the working age population will increase by about 15 million per year, and every day over this period about 33 000 young men and women will enter the labour force. They will be looking for employment that can lift them out of poverty and allow them to live a better life than their parents did (UNFPA, 2014). An estimated 600 million jobs will need to be created worldwide by 2025 in order to keep current employment rates at their current level (ILO, 2012a). Over the next two decades, 440 million young people in sub-Saharan Africa will be entering the labour market looking for work (World Bank/IFAD, 2017).

Overall, young people live for the most part in rural settings, but large disparities are observed across world regions and countries' levels of economic development. In 2015, the rural population was estimated to reach about 65% of the overall population in South-Central Asia, and 62% in sub-Saharan Africa (UNDESA, 2015). While the proportion of rural youth has declined since 1950, its absolute number is expected to increase in sub-Saharan Africa and decrease in Asia (UNFPA, 2014). The countries with the highest proportion of rural youth can be found in the Horn of Africa, the Sahel and in Southern Asia. Data from 24 School-to-Work Transition Survey (SWTS) countries[1] spanning the period 2012 15 reveal that the average proportion of rural dwellers among youth stands at 54.0% (Figure 1.2).

Figure 1.2. Distribution of youth by area of residence, %

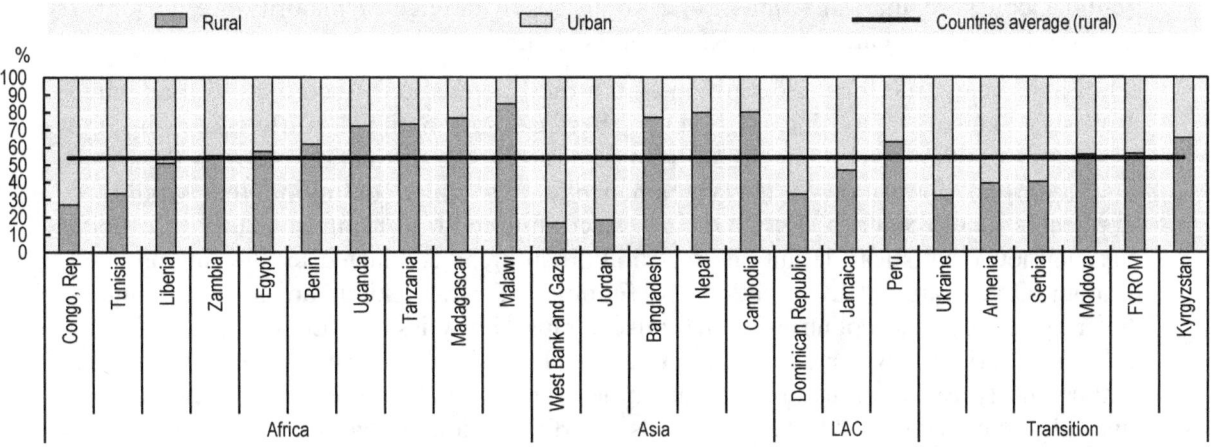

1. Youth are aged 15-29.
2. The survey was conducted in 2012 for Peru; 2013 for Bangladesh, Dominican Republic, Kyrgyzstan, Nepal, Tanzania and Tunisia; 2014 for Armenia, Benin, Cambodia, Egypt, Former Yugoslav Republic of Macedonia (FYROM), Liberia, Malawi and Zambia; and 2015 for Congo (Republic of the), Jamaica, Jordan, Madagascar, Moldova, Serbia, Uganda, Ukraine, and West Bank and Gaza Strip.
3. Of the 32 available countries, 8 were excluded: Lebanon, Montenegro, Togo and Viet Nam because sampling weights were missing; Colombia and El Salvador because data are representative for the urban population only; and Brazil and the Russian Federation because data do not cover all regions and therefore are not nationally representative.
4. Countries average refers to the simple arithmetic (unweighted) mean of all countries displayed.
Source: Authors' own calculations based on ILO's School-to-Work Transition Survey data from 2012 to 2015.

The situation does not seem to have evolved much from early 1990s when rural youth accounted for around 55% of the world youth population (FAO, 1991). The share of youth living in rural areas reaches very high levels in sub-Saharan Africa and Asia (84.7% in Malawi, 79.8% in Cambodia and 79.5% in Nepal), whereas it is markedly lower in the Middle East and North Africa (16.4% in West Bank and Gaza, and 18.2% in Jordan), in Eastern Europe and Central Asia (EECA) (32.3% in Ukraine and 39.3% in Armenia), and in Latin America and the Caribbean (33.0% in the Dominican Republic and 46.7% in Jamaica). In other words, in low-income economies (all located in sub-Saharan Africa and Asia) most youth live in rural areas, while the reverse is true for youth in upper-middle income group.[2] This mirrors the fact that as countries reach higher levels of income and urbanise, the fertility rate declines (Elder et al., 2015).

While the youth population living in rural areas represents a majority in developing and emerging countries, and an even larger constituency in low-income countries, the definition of "rural youth" varies across the world. The United Nations defines "youth" as those persons between the ages of 15 and 24 years, while the African Union defines it as those between the ages of 10 and 35. The age definition varies between countries as well, from 12-30 years in Nigeria to 18-35 in Uganda, 16-35 in Côte d'Ivoire and 16-30 in Viet Nam. But beyond age, the "youth" and "rural youth" are categories that bring together a diversity of characteristics and vulnerabilities. Youth is not a homogeneous group and needs refinement in order to reflect the diverse and complex realities in which young people live, inform policy makers and help young people access opportunities. For example, youth aged 15-17 – below the legal age of majority – may encounter more barriers in accessing resources, services, employment opportunities, and markets than older youth. In rural areas especially, they face greater risks to engage in harmful jobs (child labour). At the same time, older youth above the age of majority are no longer covered by the Convention on the Rights of the Child.

The same holds true for the definition of the rural population. According to the United Nations Statistics Division (UNSD), "because of national differences in the characteristics that distinguish urban from rural areas, the distinction between the urban and the rural population is not yet amenable to a single definition that would be applicable to all countries" (UNSD, n.d.). According to an in-depth inventory of official national-level statistical definitions for rural/urban areas conducted by the International Labour Organization (ILO), national definitions of rural and urban areas are highly heterogeneous across countries, which raise comparability issues (ILO, n.d.). Definitions rely on criteria as diverse as population size and density, administrative and legal area, settlement type, infrastructure and amenities, and predominance of agricultural/non-agricultural activities, for instance. It is also worth mentioning that in the vast majority of cases rural areas are defined as a residual, i.e. all areas not classified as urban.

Moving from childhood to youth is a major transition that witnesses many changes, from the evolution of power dynamics to changing social and economic dependency relationships towards greater responsibilities and new forms of individual aspirations. In particular, aspirations are thought to be one of the aspects that influence livelihoods choices and strategies, and should be considered when analysing young people's engagement in the world of work (Sumberg et al., 2014; OECD, 2017). In the same manner, rural young people experience very diverse social and spatial realities that will influence the way they engage in employment, including the level of education and skills, gender, location (diversity of rural areas and abundance of natural resources), social norms, social networks, family poverty level, and access to assets such as land, finance and knowledge.

Rural youth in developing countries are low educated and the majority work in poor-quality jobs

The potential for rural young people to build their social and economic capital and independence is undermined by a set of challenges. Young people in rural areas face the double challenge of age-specific vulnerabilities and underdevelopment of rural areas. Such challenges include low access to quality education and vocational training, assets such as land and finance, and limited opportunities to participate in decision-making. Young women face additional constraints resulting from discriminatory social institutions (OECD Development Centre, 2014), in particular, a high time burden resulting from their productive and reproductive responsibilities, and in certain countries limited mobility, all of which limit their employment opportunities. This chapter provides an overview of common rural youth challenges.

One in five rural youth never attended school

Educational attainment is low among youth in rural areas. Nearly one-fifth (18.5%) of rural youth have never attended school and almost half of them (48.0%) have at best completed primary education (Figure 1.3). Rural youth are less likely to undertake vocational education (10.7%) or tertiary education (10.5%). Urban youth do clearly better with respect to educational attainment. A large majority go beyond primary school to complete higher levels of education – 33.3% in general secondary education, 11.5% in vocational secondary education, and 18.1% in tertiary education; those who never entered formal schooling account for just 12.5%. Rural youth have the poorest educational backgrounds in sub-Saharan African countries and in low-income economies. In Liberia, Malawi and Uganda, for instance, around half of the rural youth population never went to school and less than 1% had the chance to complete tertiary studies. Rural youth educational attainment can greatly diverge across countries. In West Bank and Gaza, as many as 59.1% of rural youth are uneducated. At the other end of the spectrum, 54.8% of rural youth in Ukraine have a tertiary education.

Figure 1.3. Distribution of rural youth by highest level of education completed, %

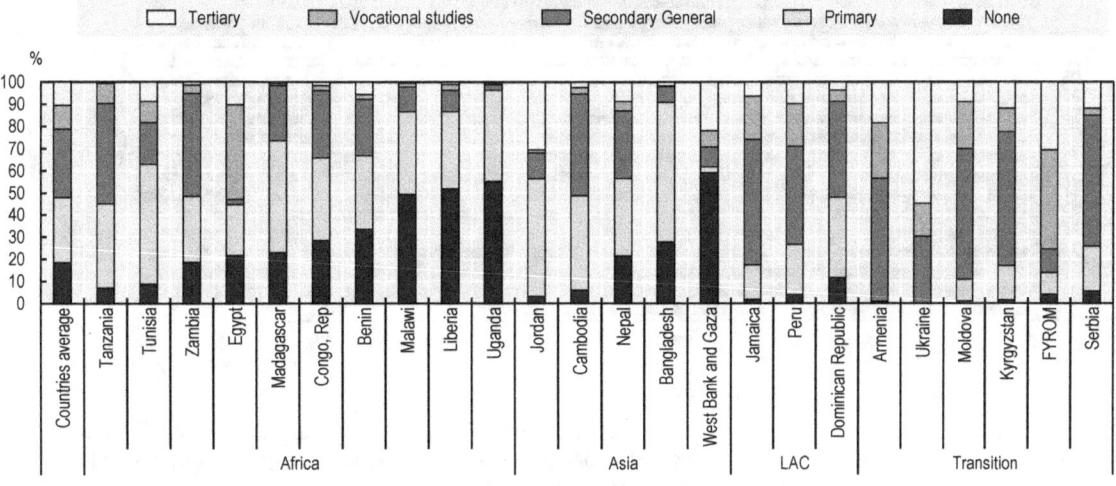

1. See Notes 1-4 of Figure 1.2.
Source: Authors' own calculations based on ILO's School-to-Work Transition Survey data from 2012 to 2015.

Agriculture is the main provider of jobs for rural youth. This sector of activity accounts on average for 36.6% of rural youth employment, far ahead of manufacturing and construction, trade and transportation, and other services, which employ, respectively, 17.9%, 23.7% and 21.7% of rural young workers (Figure 1.4). Low-income economies are characterised by the lack of employment opportunities outside agriculture. Most of these countries are located in sub-Saharan Africa.[3] The majority of rural youth are engaged in agricultural activities in Nepal (51.4%), Cambodia (55.2%), Kyrgyzstan (61.6%), Liberia (63.3%), Malawi (63.9%), Uganda (70.9%) and especially Madagascar, where they are close to four in five (79.1%). The share of rural youth working in manufacturing and construction is as low as 9.7% in Uganda, 9.1% in Madagascar and

8.2% in Liberia, suggesting that in these countries agro-processing industries are still significantly underdeveloped.

The picture is slightly different in the Asia-Pacific region, where the manufacturing sector has been expanding. The decline in the number of young farmers mirrors various sociological and demographic trends and phenomena, including urbanisation and outmigration. Almost half of the population of the Asia-Pacific region now lives in urban areas and the urbanisation trends are accelerating (FAO, 2015). In addition, the demand for jobs in sectors such as manufacturing and construction is leading to a contraction of employment in agriculture. Manufacturing accounts for more than a quarter of total youth employment in Cambodia, and one-fifth in Indonesia (ILO, 2015). According to the SWTS data, the share of rural youth working in manufacturing reaches 21.6% in Cambodia and 28.6% in Bangladesh (Figure 1.4).

Figure 1.4. Distribution of rural young workers by sector of activity, %

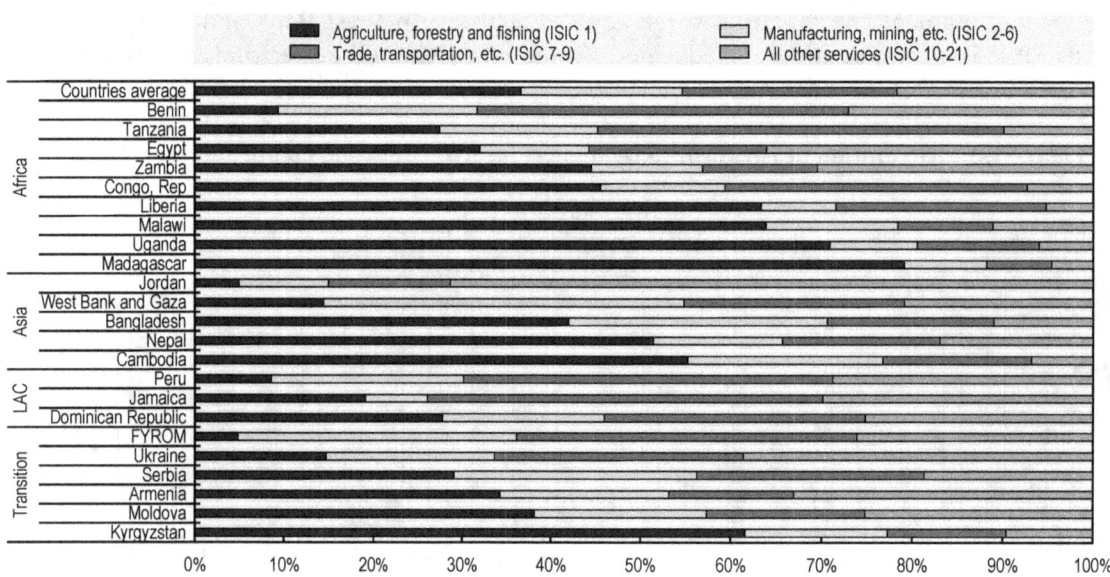

1. See Notes 1-4 of Figure 1.2.
2. Based on the International Standard Industry Classification (ISIC), industries are aggregated in four categories: agriculture, forestry and fishing (ISIC 1); manufacturing, mining, electricity and water supply related activities and construction (ISIC 2-6); wholesale and retail trade, repair, transportation and storage, accommodation and food services activities (ISIC 7-9); and other services activities including information, communication, finance, real estate, administrative services, education, etc. (ISIC 10-21).
3. Data are missing for Tunisia.
Source: Authors' own calculations based on ILO's School-to-Work Transition Survey data from 2012 to 2015.

Rural youth are predominantly in vulnerable employment

Self-employed workers (employers, own-account workers and co-operative members) and contributing family workers together outnumber wage employees. Among the 23 SWTS countries that have information on employment status, wage employment accounts on average for 47.0% of rural youth employment (Figure 1.5). In other words, rural young workers are predominantly self-employed (26.2%) and contributing family workers (23.2%), which are considered vulnerable employment[4] and usually a proxy for the extent of informal employment. When it comes to low-income economies and sub-Saharan African countries, the share of paid employees among rural young workers falls dramatically, and is as low as 5.8% in Liberia and 10.4% in Madagascar. Self-employment becomes the dominant employment segment, and a large number of rural youth appear to perform productive activities as contributing family workers.

Figure 1.5. Distribution of rural young workers by employment status, %

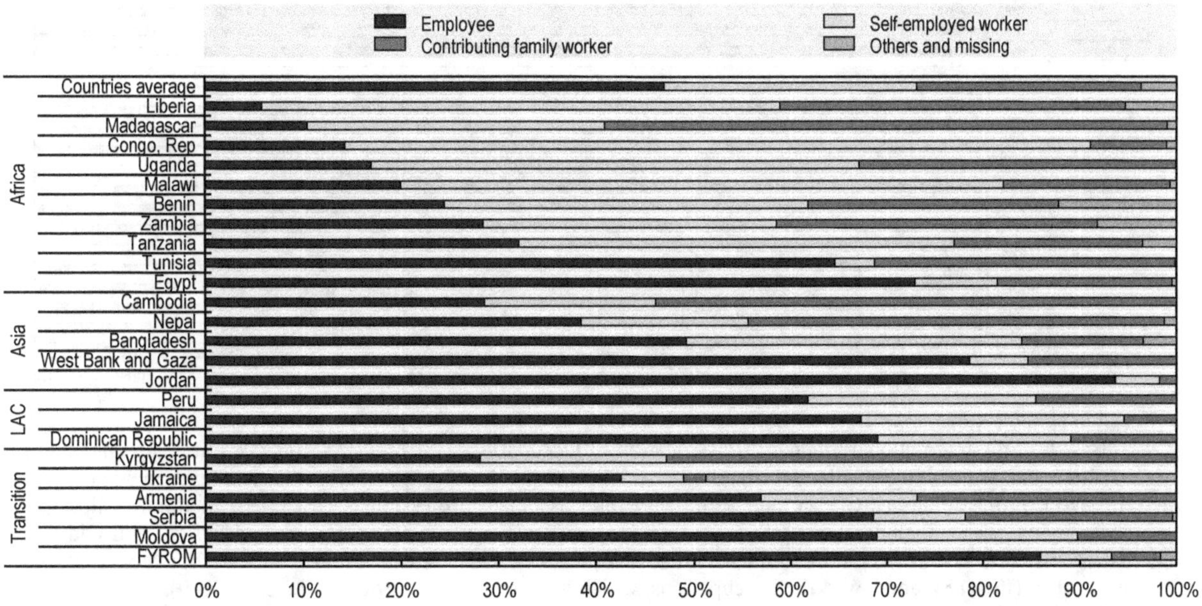

1. See Notes 1-4 of Figure 1.2.
2. The SWTS generic questionnaire provides information about the employment status of young workers by asking them to describe their job/activity among the following categories: employee (working for someone else for pay in cash or in kind), employer (employing one or more employees), own-account worker (not employing any employee), member of a producers' co-operative, helping without pay in the business or farm of another household/family member. Due to the relatively low sample size for some of these options (employer, co-operative member) and to differences across countries, we aggregated these categories into three groups: wage employees, self-employed (including employers, own-account workers and co-operative members) and unpaid family workers (corresponding to helping without pay).
Source: Authors' own calculations based on ILO's School-to-Work Transition Survey data from 2012 to 2015.

Given the large number of rural youth concentrated in vulnerable employment and agricultural activities, which are generally characterised in developing countries by low productivity and earnings and poor working conditions, it is not surprising that very few rural young workers occupy high-skilled positions. On average, high-skilled occupations account for no more than 12.5% of rural youth employment (Figure 1.6). Rural young workers in low-skilled occupations – i.e. elementary occupations – are not more numerous (16.0%). The majority of rural youth are in medium-skilled occupations (71.5%), which range from clerical support (non-manual labour) to agriculture and factory workers (manual). Again, these global findings mask large disparities across regions and countries. In low-income economies and sub-Saharan African countries, a very small percentage of rural young workers are engaged in high-skilled occupations (e.g. 1.5% in Madagascar, 2.5% in Liberia, 2.8% in Uganda). On the other hand, more than a quarter of rural young workers are in high-skilled jobs in Jordan (26.0%) and FYROM (27.3%), and more than one-third of rural young workers are in high-skilled jobs in Ukraine (37.4%). These are developing countries belonging to the middle-income group.

Figure 1.6. Distribution of rural young workers by occupation, %

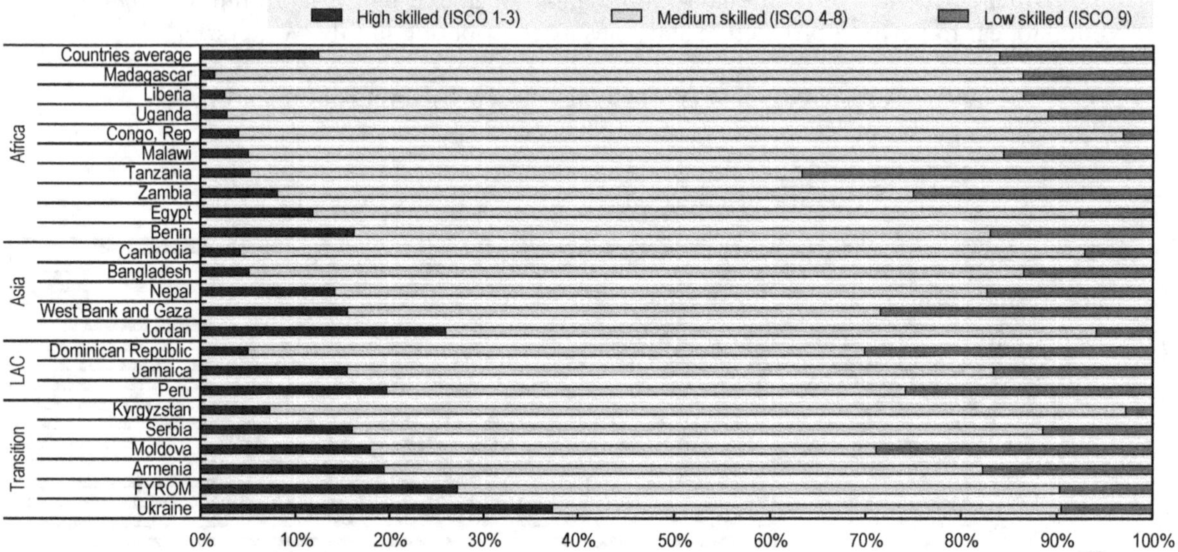

Legend: High skilled (ISCO 1-3); Medium skilled (ISCO 4-8); Low skilled (ISCO 9)

Countries (grouped by region):
- **Africa**: Countries average, Madagascar, Liberia, Uganda, Congo Rep., Malawi, Tanzania, Zambia, Egypt, Benin
- **Asia**: Cambodia, Bangladesh, Nepal, West Bank and Gaza, Jordan
- **LAC**: Dominican Republic, Jamaica, Peru
- **Transition**: Kyrgyzstan, Serbia, Moldova, Armenia, FYROM, Ukraine

1. See Notes 1-4 of Figure 1.2.
2. Based on the International Standard Classification of Occupations (ISCO-08), occupations are aggregated in three categories: high-skilled occupations, which include legislators, senior officials and managers (ISCO 1), professionals (ISCO 2), and technicians and associate professionals (ISCO 3); medium-skilled occupations, which include clerks (ISCO 4), service and sales workers (ISCO 5), skilled agricultural and fishery workers (ISCO 6), craft and related trades workers (ISCO 7), and plant and machine operators and assemblers (ISCO 8); and low-skilled occupations, which include elementary occupations (ISCO 9).
3. Data are missing for Tunisia.

Source: Authors' own calculations based on ILO's School-to-Work Transition Survey data from 2012 to 2015.

Table 1.1. Structure of International Standard Classification of Occupations (ISCO) and broad occupation groups

Code	Major ISCO groups	Broad occupation groups
1	Managers (Chief Executives, Senior Officials and Legislators; Administrative and Commercial Managers; Production and Specialized Services Managers; Hospitality, Retail and Other Services Managers)	
2	Professionals (Science and Engineering Professionals; Health Professionals; Teaching Professionals; Business and Administration Professionals; Information and Communications Technology Professionals; Legal, Social and Cultural Professionals)	High-skilled
3	Technicians and associate professionals (Science and Engineering Associate Professionals; Health Associate Professionals; Business and Administration Associate Professionals; Legal, Social, Cultural and Related Associate Professionals; Information and Communications Technicians)	
4	Clerical support workers (General and Keyboard Clerks; Customer Services Clerks; Numerical and Material Recording Clerks; Other Clerical Support Workers)	
5	Services and sales workers (Personal Services Workers; Sales Workers; Personal Care Workers; Protective Services Workers)	
6	Skilled agricultural and fisheries workers (Market-oriented Skilled Agricultural Workers; Market-oriented Skilled Forestry, Fishery and Hunting Workers; Subsistence Farmers, Fishers, Hunters and Gatherers)	Medium-skilled
7	Craft and related trade workers (Building and Related Trades Workers (excluding Electricians); Metal, Machinery and Related Trades Workers; Handicraft and Printing Workers; Electrical and Electronic Trades Workers; Food Processing, Woodworking, Garment and Other Craft and Related Trades Workers)	
8	Plant and machine operators and assemblers (Stationary Plant and Machine Operators; Assemblers; Drivers and Mobile Plant Operators)	
9	Elementary occupations (Cleaners and Helpers; Agricultural, Forestry and Fishery Labourers; Labourers in Mining, Construction, Manufacturing and Transport; Food Preparation Assistants; Street and Related Sales and Services Workers; Refuse Workers and Other Elementary Workers)	Low-skilled

Source: ILO (2012b), International Standard Classification of Occupations (ISCO-08), Volume 1: Structure, Group Definitions and Correspondence Tables.

The reality of the labour market does not live up to rural youth aspirations

The importance of subjective measures of the quality of jobs, such as job satisfaction, is largely underestimated in developing countries. Putting youth employment preferences at the forefront of the analysis allows understanding of the nature of youth career aspirations and job-related drivers of job satisfaction (OECD, 2017). It can cast light on the discrepancies between youth expectations and the reality of the labour market and direct policy actions to narrow these gaps. Failing to meet youth aspirations will fuel frustration, lower productivity and even put social cohesion at risk. Rural youth are no exception.

The majority of rural youth want to change their current jobs

When asked about work satisfaction, most rural youth – 74.6% in the sample of countries – answered being (somewhat or very) satisfied with their main job (Figure 1.7). There are large differences across countries, however. The lowest levels of job satisfaction among rural youth are found in low-income economies and sub-Saharan African countries. Still, in only two countries rural youth are predominantly dissatisfied with their main job (Nepal with a satisfaction level of 38.2% and Tunisia with a satisfaction level of 43.0%). Overall, young workers are relatively more satisfied with their main job in urban areas (76.3% on average across surveyed countries). The area gap in job satisfaction is particularly significant in Nepal and Tunisia where, in sharp contrast with rural settings, cities exhibit a large majority of young workers satisfied with their main job (58.3% and 71.2%, respectively).

Figure 1.7. Share of satisfied rural young workers, using a raw and adjusted measure, %

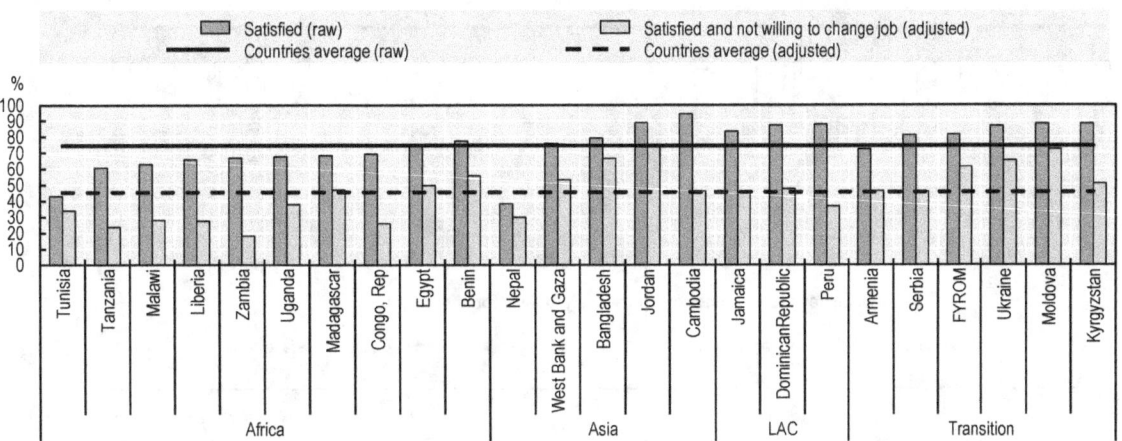

1. See Notes 1-4 of Figure 1.2.
2. The subjective measure of job satisfaction in SWTS data is measured by asking young workers to what extent they are satisfied with their main job. They can select the following options: very satisfied, somewhat satisfied, somewhat unsatisfied, and very unsatisfied. Additionally, the questionnaire includes a yes/no question about the attitude of young workers regarding their job, asking them whether they would like to change their current employment situation. The adjusted measure of satisfaction used in this report combined both variables to construct a dummy variable equal to 1 if a young worker is very or somewhat satisfied and not wanting to change jobs, and 0 when this is not case.
Source: Authors' own calculations based on ILO's School-to-Work Transition Survey data from 2012 to 2015.

Using an adjusted measure of job satisfaction that takes into account only satisfied workers who do not want to change their current employment situation shows a different picture, however. When using this adjusted measure, the level of job satisfaction among rural youth falls from 74.6% to 45.3% on average (Figure 1.7). In other words, more than half of rural young workers want to change jobs. The same holds true for urban youth, although the adjusted measure of job satisfaction is not quite as low (47.4%).

Whatever the level of job satisfaction expressed, on average, half (50.2%) of rural young workers would like to change their current employment situation (Figure 1.8 Panel A), and one-quarter (25.7%) are actively looking for another job (Figure 1.8 Panel B). In urban areas, young workers are less likely to be willing to change job (49.0%) but, on the other hand, in terms looking for another job, they are relatively more numerous (28.2%). The proportion of rural youth willing to change job is particularly high in sub-Saharan African countries, most of which are low-income economies. For instance, it stands at 58.7% in Uganda, 65.8% in Malawi, 68.2% in Liberia, 71.5% in Tanzania and Congo (Republic of the), and 77.8% in Zambia. However, more economically advanced countries in other regions also exhibit a large proportion of rural youth willing to change jobs (53.7% in Cambodia, 57.7% in Tunisia, 61.7% in Peru and 61.8% in Jamaica). MENA countries accounts, in addition, for very high shares (well above countries average) of rural youth actively looking for another job (42.7% in Jordan, 44.3% in Tunisia and 46.8% in West Bank and Gaza).

Figure 1.8. Share of rural youth willing to change job and actively looking for another job, %

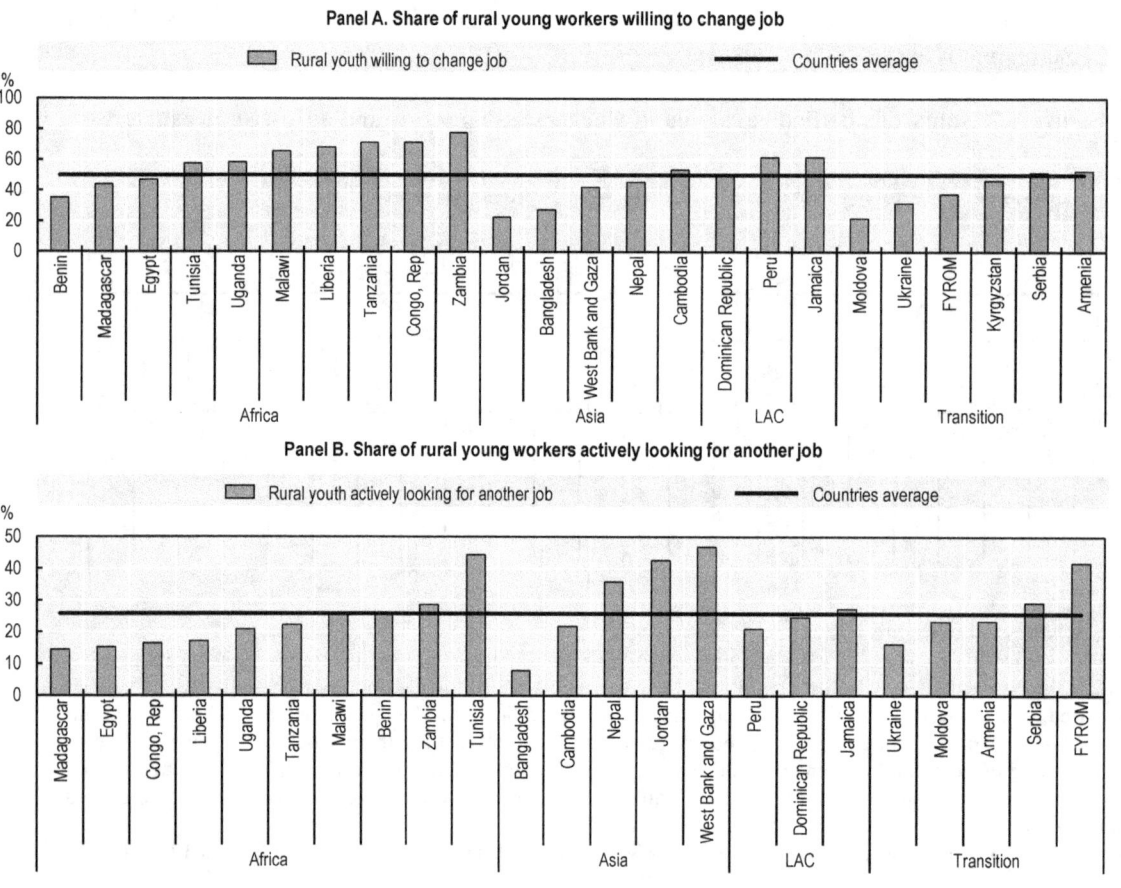

1. See Notes 1-4 of Figure 1.2.
2. Panel B data are missing for Kyrgyzstan.
Source: Authors' own calculations based on ILO's School-to-Work Transition Survey data from 2012 to 2015.

Rural youth working in agriculture want better working conditions

Why is it then that so many rural young workers are willing to change their current employment situation? Evidence from the SWTS shows that by and large the main reason stated for wanting to change jobs is low pay. More than one-third (36.7%) of rural young workers want to change job to secure a better income (Figure 1.9). This mirrors the low productivity levels of the jobs available to youth in rural areas. The second most cited reason (20.1%) is because their current job is of a temporary nature. Stable employment is usually less frequent in rural areas where economic activities are seasonal and/or more dependent on the primary sector and therefore highly vulnerable to external shocks (e.g. weather conditions and natural hazards). Poor working conditions and skills mismatch are other reasons that push a significant proportion of rural youth to look for another job (17.1% and 13.3%, respectively). The same findings are observed in urban areas, albeit urban youth willing to change job seem to care less about working conditions (15.2%) and more by a pay increase (39.4%) than their rural peers. The results disaggregated by sector of activity further show that in agriculture, rural youth willing to change job are less attracted by a better pay (33.9%) and are more interested in having better working conditions (19.3%) than in other sectors (41.1% and 15.2%, respectively, in manufacturing for instance). These findings are in line with the situation generally observed in developing countries, according to which most rural youth engage in subsistence activities, primarily in agriculture, since employment opportunities are scarce outside this sector; moreover, rural youth are faced with working conditions that are often far from decent.

Figure 1.9. Distribution of rural young workers willing to change job, by reason and sector of activity, %

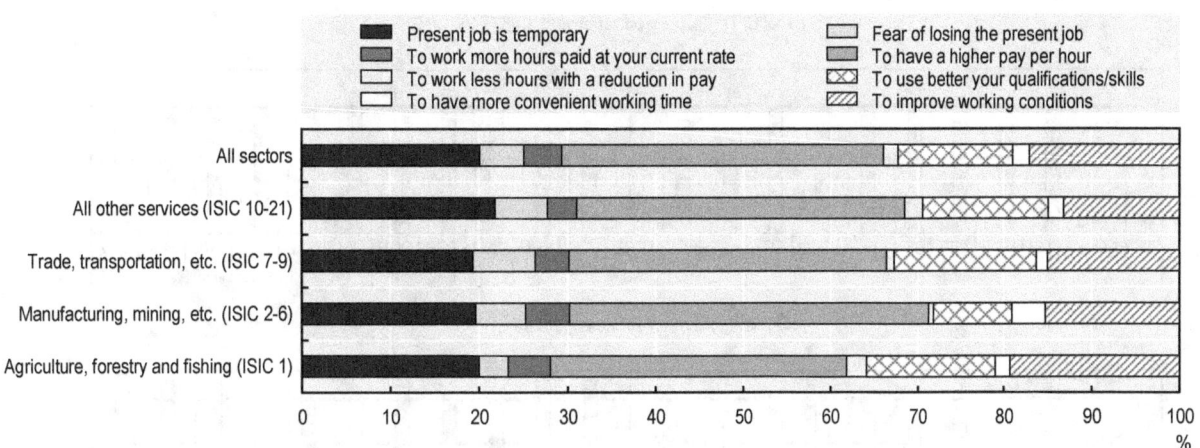

1. See Notes 1-4 of Figure 1.2.
2. Countries' average displayed.
3. Data are missing for Tunisia.
Source: Authors' own calculations based on ILO's School-to-Work Transition Survey data from 2012 to 2015.

Rural youth working in agriculture are the least satisfied

Job satisfaction data further point to the challenge of making agricultural employment attractive for young people. Rural young workers are without doubt the least satisfied in the agricultural sector which, beyond agriculture, also encompasses forestry and fishery, and thus can be assimilated into the primary sector of the economy.[5] Only 68.7% of rural young workers are (very or somewhat) satisfied with their main job in agriculture, in contrast with 78.5% in manufacturing and construction, 77.1% in trade and transportation, and 82.1% in all other services (Figure 1.10).

Figure 1.10. Share of satisfied rural young workers by sector of activity, %

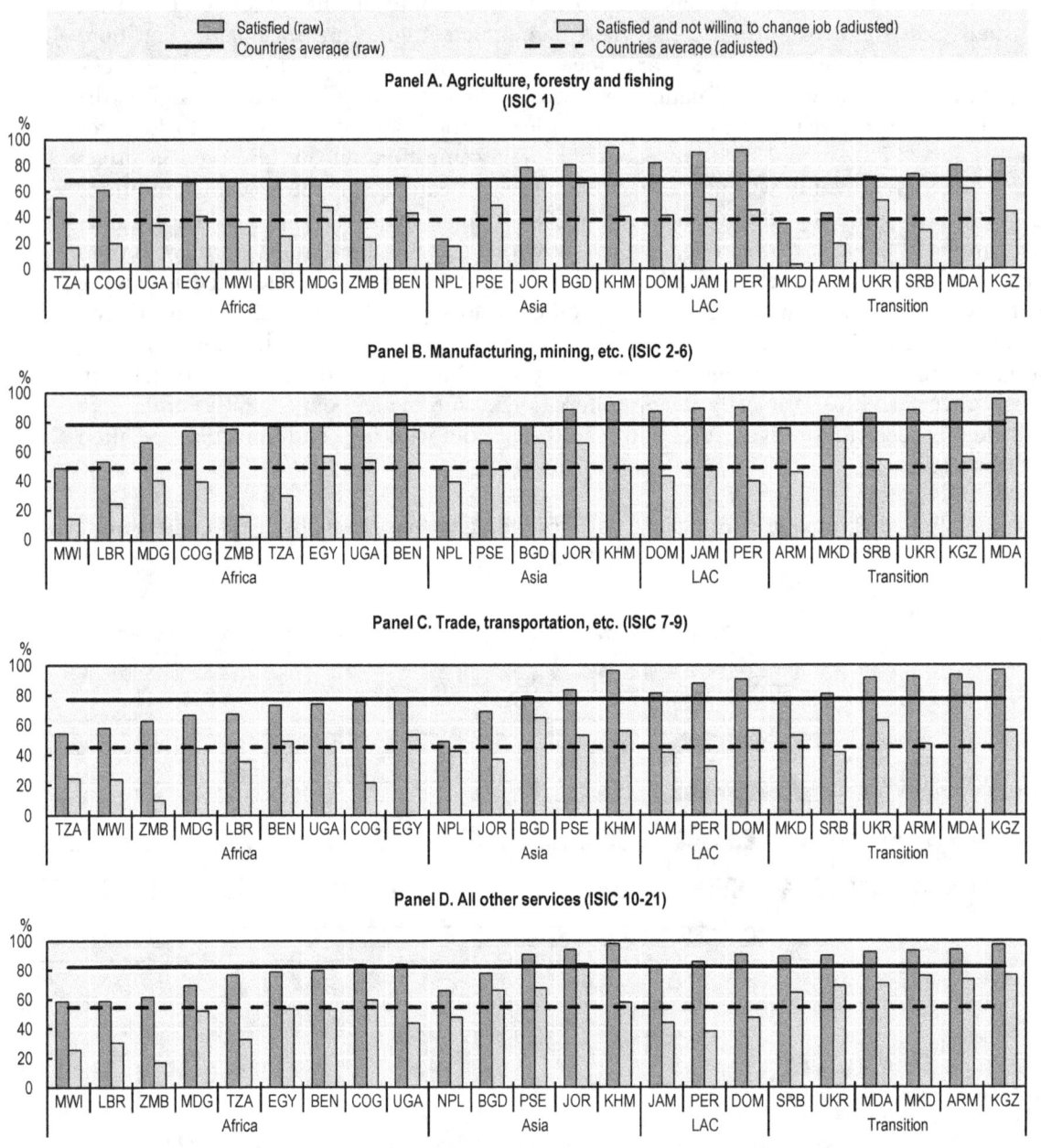

1. See Notes 1-2 of Figure 1.7.
2. Data are missing for Tunisia.
Source: Authors' own calculations based on ILO's School-to-Work Transition Survey data from 2012 to 2015.

When applying the adjusted measure of satisfaction, barely 37.8% of rural young workers are satisfied and not willing to change job in agriculture, far less than in the other sectors, which reach 48.9% in manufacturing and construction, 45.3% in trade and transportation and 54.5% in all other services. In some countries, and not only in low-income economies where agriculture is basically at subsistence level, rudimentary and less productive, discontent about agriculture is incredibly widespread. For instance, in Nepal and FYROM the raw measure of job satisfaction in agriculture amounts to only 22.5% and 34.3%, and the adjusted measure to barely 17.1% and 3.1%, respectively. Moreover, less than 20% of rural youth in agriculture is satisfied and not willing to change job in Tanzania (16.4%), Armenia (19.2%) and the Republic of the Congo (19.6%). The poor quality of employment in agriculture in developing countries not only affects rural youth workers' standard of living but also hinders their subjective well-being.

A persistent high level of job dissatisfaction among youth in agriculture fosters rural outmigration. In the absence of decent work opportunities in rural areas, migration is and will continue to be one of the options to escape poverty and find more and better job opportunities. Evidence that a large proportion of migrants are rural people can be deduced from the fact that around 40% of international remittances are sent to rural areas (World Bank, 2014). About one-third of all international migrants are young, aged between 15 and 34 (FAO, 2016). Migration can be seasonal or temporary between rural areas for agricultural jobs. It could also be for longer periods to cities or other countries. In many parts of Asia and Africa, remittances from migration outweigh the income from agriculture. One of the most significant changes in the last half century is the increasing proportion of women migrating: today, they constitute half of the international migrant population, often migrating independently as the main economic providers for their families (FAO, 2010). In Asia, 46% of all migrants between 10 and 24 years of age are female.

Migration can be a positive experience for youth, often contributing to better education and greater skills development. However, it can also enhance the risk of exploitation, abuse, social exclusion, adverse health issues, human trafficking and death, with variability in risk between the sexes. Female youth, for instance, are especially vulnerable to human trafficking for sexual exploitation, while male youth are susceptible to forced labour, including in the fishing industry (UNESCAP, 2016).

Contributing family work and low-skilled occupations decrease job satisfaction

Rural youth are also the least satisfied in contributing family work and in low-skilled occupations, where employment is usually of very low quality. Contributing family work is by definition classified as informal employment, which sheds light on the poor quality of this employment status. Contributing family workers are workers who hold self-employment jobs in an establishment operated by a related person, with too limited a degree of involvement in its operation to be considered a partner (ILO, 1993). Contributing family workers are most of the time unpaid family helpers. Based on the raw measure of job satisfaction, the data show that, among rural youth, 68.0% of contributing family workers are satisfied with their employment situation, compared with 75.5% of paid employees and 76.7% of self-employed workers (Figure 1.11). Disparities in job satisfaction levels are also notable when using the adjusted measure. Contributing family workers are barely more than one-third (36.1%) likely to be satisfied and not willing to change job. By contrast, paid employees and self-employed workers are, respectively, 46.7% and 48.7% more likely to be satisfied and not willing to change job. Apart from Moldova (50.2%), Jordan (59.2%) and especially Bangladesh (67.3%), in all countries rural young contributing family workers are a minority in terms of being satisfied and not willing to change job, a minority which is very tiny in poorer countries such as Nepal

(9.9%), Tanzania (19.6%) and Zambia (20.18%), or in transition countries such as FYROM (24.6%) and Armenia (24.8%).

Figure 1.11. **Share of satisfied rural young workers by employment status, %**

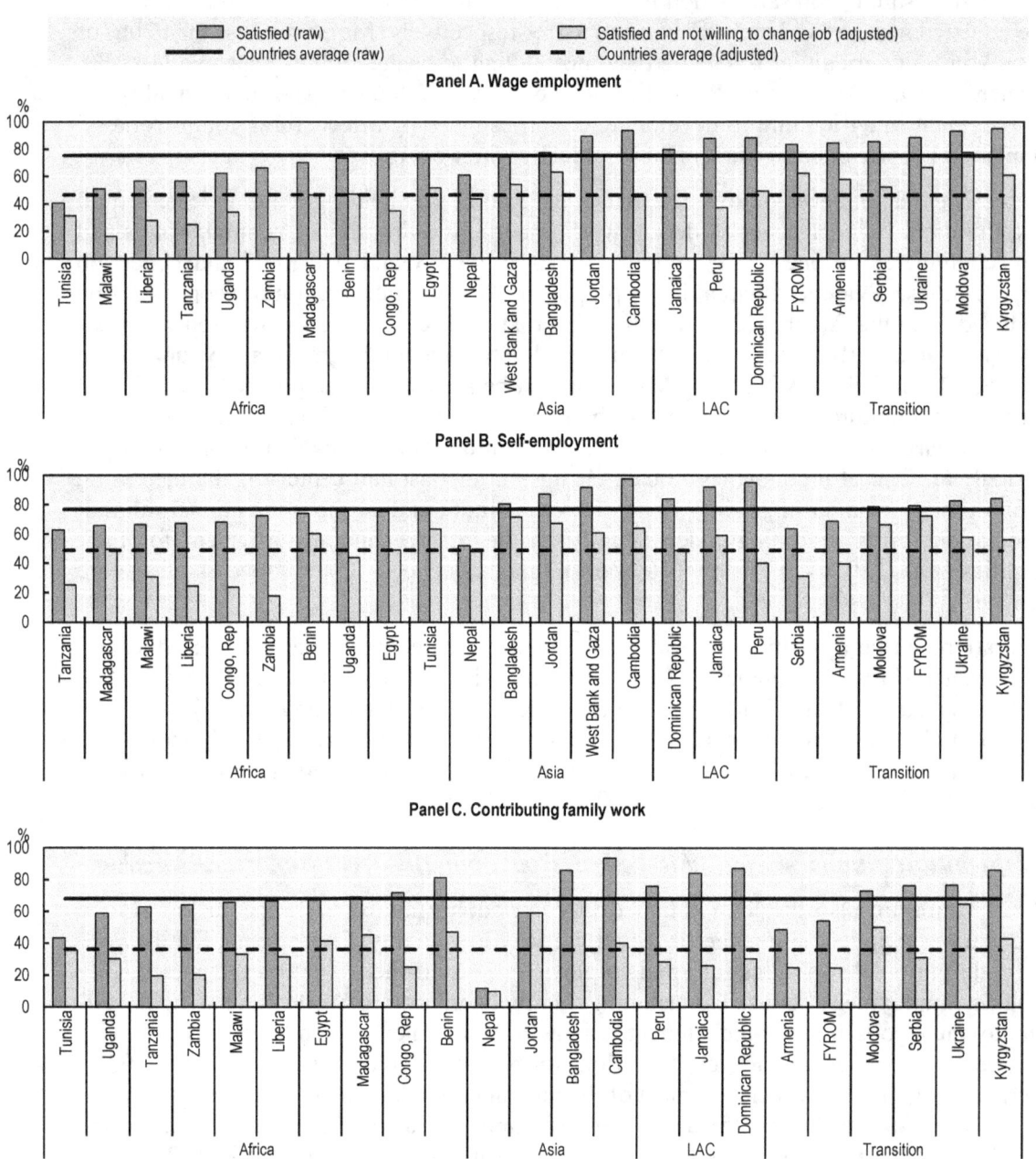

1. See Notes 1-2 of Figure 1.7.
2. Panel C data are missing for West Bank and Gaza.
Source: Authors' own calculations based on ILO's School-to-Work Transition Survey data from 2012 to 2015.

Likewise, the lower the level of skills required for the occupation, the less satisfied rural young workers are. This is very apparent in Figure 1.12. While rural young workers are, on average, 85.9% (very or somewhat) satisfied with their employment situation in high-skilled occupations, they are just 75.6% satisfied in medium-skilled occupations and

67.8% satisfied in low-skilled (elementary) occupations. Similarly, according to the adjusted measure, it appears that rural young workers are, on average, 58.1% satisfied and not willing to change jobs in high-skilled occupations. The corresponding figures for medium- and low-skilled occupations are 45.2% and 36.9%, respectively. Elementary occupations, by definition, do not require a skilled workforce and therefore correspond to low-productivity activities that provide low pay and worse working conditions, including occupational safety and health-related matters. Based on the adjusted measure, some countries, mainly low-income sub-Saharan African economies, raise high concern given their extremely low levels of job satisfaction among rural young workers in low-skilled occupations, such as Tanzania (26.2%), Malawi (19.8%), Zambia (18.0%) and especially the Republic of the Congo (1.3%), where job dissatisfaction affects the quasi-totality of the rural youth employed population in elementary occupations. In these countries and in other low-income economies such as Nepal (24.2%) and Liberia (26.9%), job discontent, as defined by the adjusted measure, is widespread among medium-skilled occupations as well. By contrast, overall, the majority of rural youth occupied in high-skilled positions are satisfied and not willing to change jobs, except in a few countries – Malawi (21.8%), Jamaica (36.8%), Peru (40.1%), Zambia (40.3%) and Liberia (47.5%). The research findings presented thus far clearly show the close link between the quality of employment and job satisfaction. It would be difficult to convince rural young to keep their jobs if these do not permit them to make a living and have decent lives.

Figure 1.12. Share of satisfied rural young workers by occupation, %

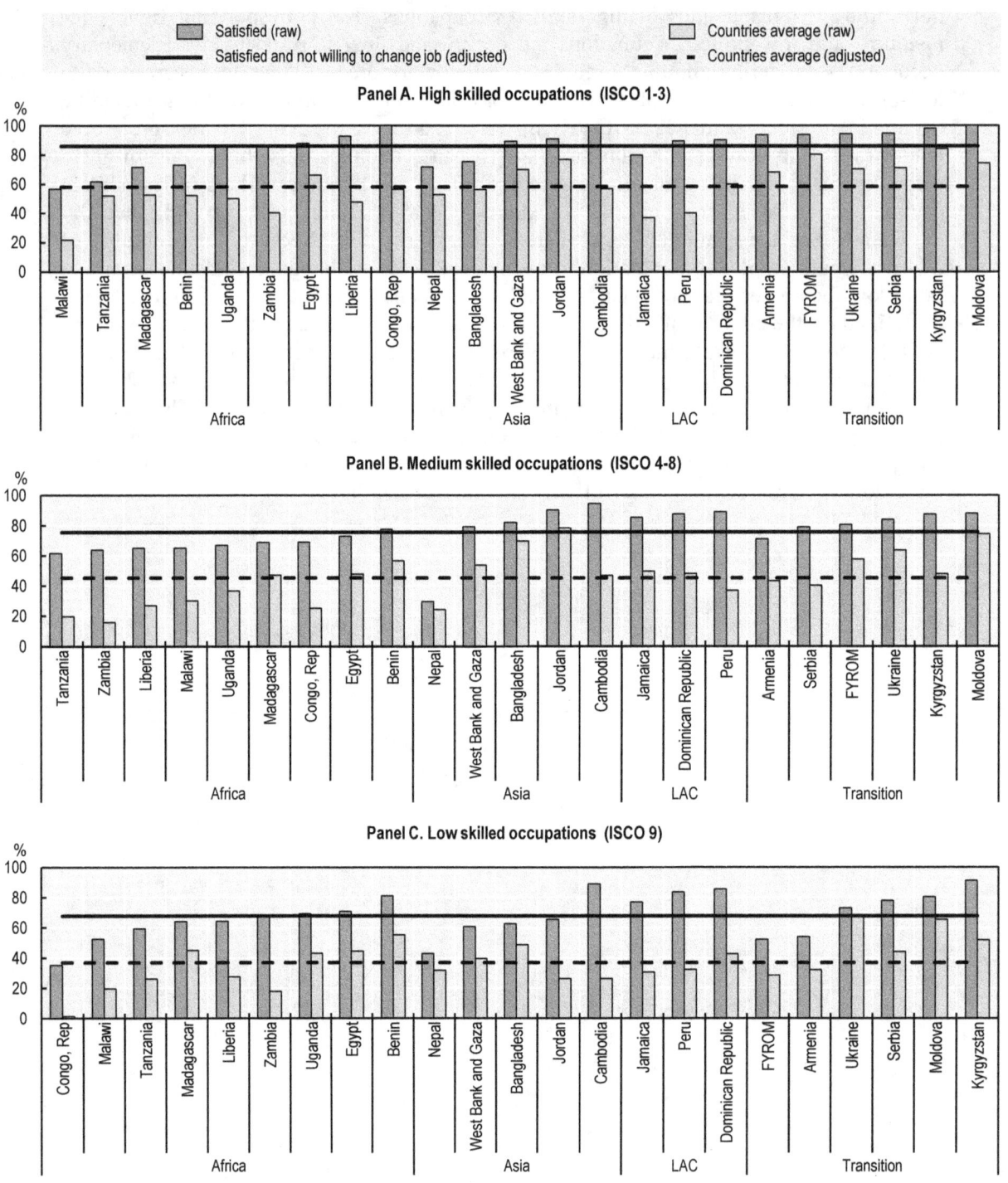

1. See Notes 1-2 of Figure 1.7.
2. Data are missing for Tunisia.
Source: Authors' own calculations based on ILO's School-to-Work Transition Survey data from 2012 to 2015.

Most rural students aspire to work in high-skilled occupations, yet very few rural young workers access them

Subjective indicators, such as job satisfaction, are difficult to interpret. This is because they are not only dependent on the actual (objective) situation of individuals but are also (and most importantly perhaps) influenced by their aspirations. Results are actually often counterintuitive at first sight – individuals in better situations report lower levels of satisfaction – but they can be explained by the fact that people who fare worse tend to have lower aspirations (in particular, because they are less aware of what they could possibly get) and as a result they have fewer reasons to express dissatisfaction. Figure 1.13 reports career aspirations of rural students in terms of occupation. It would appear that the vast majority of rural students, 76.4% precisely, aspire to work in high-skilled occupations. In line with previous arguments, this number is probably overestimated, since students are likely to have higher career aspirations than out-of-school youth (they are likely to come from better-off families where parents are engaged in higher-skilled occupations). Unsurprisingly, there are very few rural students, and in many countries close to none, willing to work in elementary occupations. Students have higher career aspirations in urban areas where, overall, as many as 80.3% are likely to aspire to high-skilled positions.

Figure 1.13. Career aspirations of rural students, by occupation, %

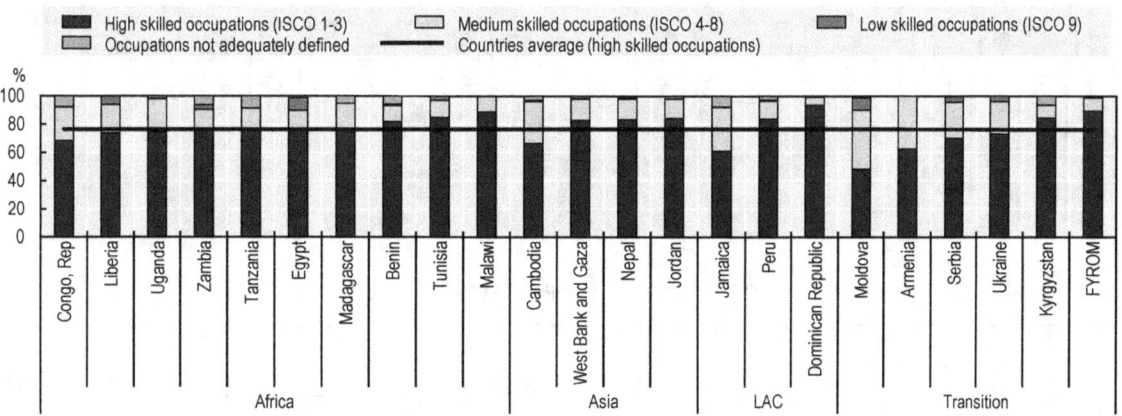

1. See Notes 1-4 of Figure 1.2.
2. Career aspirations in terms of occupation are documented in SWTS data via the question "Ideally, what type of work would you like to do?" The question is asked to 15-29 year-old students enrolled at any level of education and uses the ISCO as a reference. Students unwilling to work were discarded from the sample, as they represented a negligible proportion of individuals.
3. Data are missing for Bangladesh.
Source: Authors' own calculations based on ILO's School-to-Work Transition Survey data from 2012 to 2015.

Comparing rural students' career aspirations and the distribution of rural young workers by occupation, it appears that youth career aspiration gaps for high-skilled occupations are extremely large in rural areas. Whereas 76.4% of rural students would like to work in high-skilled occupations only 12.5% of rural young workers actually work in high-skilled occupations (Figure 1.14).

36 | CHAPTER 1. RURAL YOUTH LIVELIHOOD: A SITUATION ANALYSIS

Figure 1.14. Youth career aspiration gaps among rural youth, by occupation, %

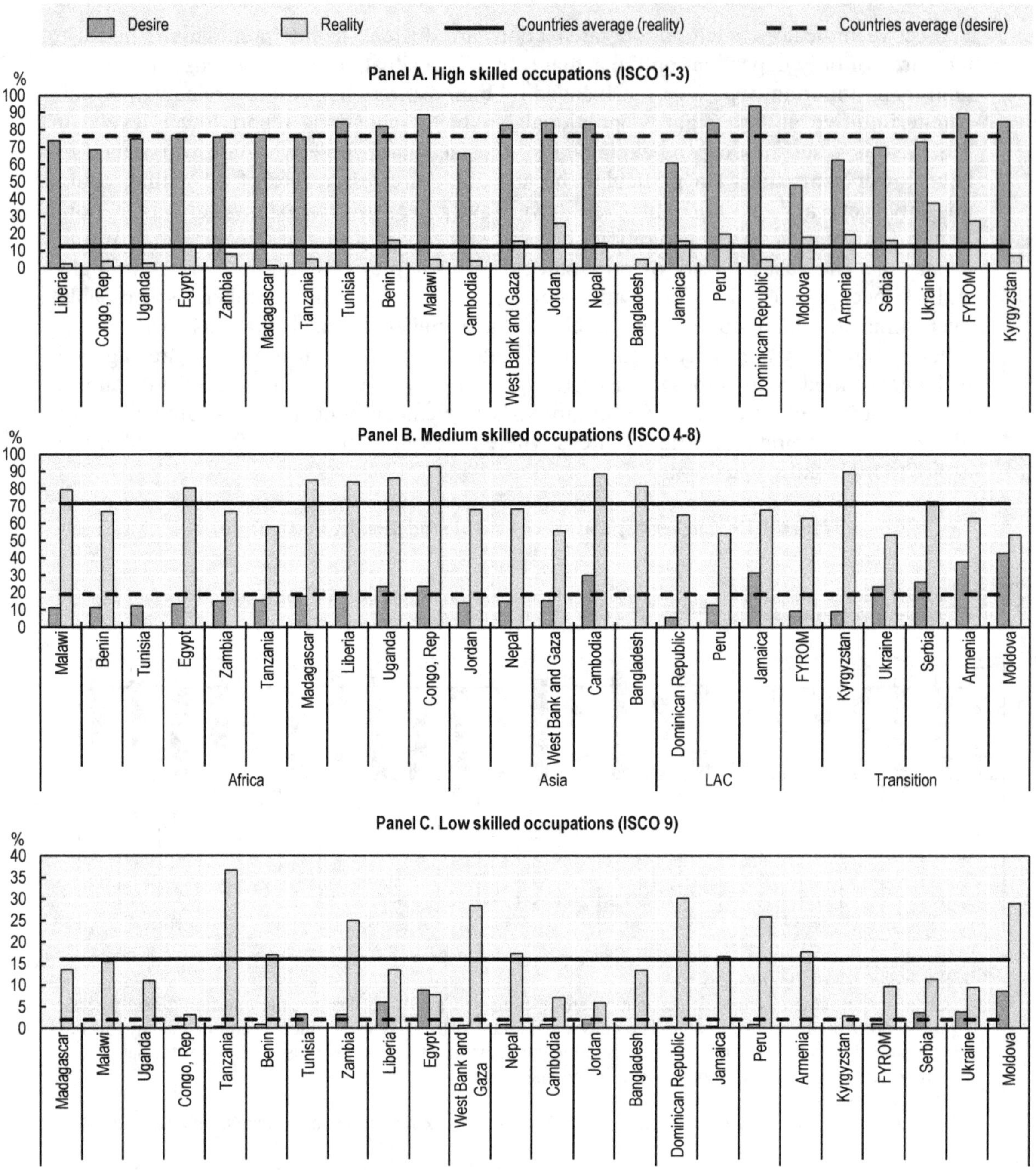

1. See Notes 1-2 of Figure 1.13.
2. "Desire" refers to career aspirations of rural students in terms of occupation, and "reality" corresponds to the occupation of rural young workers.
3. Data on career aspirations ("desire") are missing for Bangladesh, and data on occupation ("reality") are missing for Tunisia.

Source: Authors' own calculations based on ILO's School-to-Work Transition Survey data from 2012 to 2015.

As expected, for lower-skilled occupations the aspirations gaps are reversed. Only 18.9% of rural students aim to work in medium-skilled occupations, whereas the majority (71.5%) of rural young workers are in such occupations. The gap is also significant for low-skilled occupations: 2.0% (desire) versus 16.0% (reality). Compared with rural areas, the aspiration gap for high-skilled occupations is not that large in urban areas: the higher proportion of students aspiring to high-skilled positions (82.4%) is more than offset by the larger proportion of young workers occupying such positions (21.3%). On the other hand, rural youth both aspire more and actually work more in lower-skilled occupations than urban youth do, suggesting that the lack of qualified jobs in rural areas not only hampers youth access to productive employment but also lowers their occupational aspirations. In rural areas, the youth career aspiration gaps for high-skilled occupations are the largest in Madagascar (75.3 percentage points difference between desire and reality), Kyrgyzstan (77.3%), Malawi (83.6%) and the Dominican Republic (88.5%).

Skills gaps remain large in rural areas

Although most rural young workers consider themselves to have the relevant qualifications, skills mismatch and, in particular, underqualification, is a major issue. Figure 1.15 displays subjective and objective measures of skills mismatch. The subjective measure corresponds to rural young workers' perceptions about the relevance of their education to their current job requirements. In turn, the objective measure follows a normative approach based on the level of education required for each type of occupation. According to the subjective measure, the majority of rural young workers, 62.8%, consider themselves to have the relevant education (Figure 1.15 Panel A). Only 19.2% consider themselves as underqualified, and 18.0% as overqualified. Based on these subjective figures, skills mismatch does not seem to be a major issue for rural youth. This is all the more true for urban youth who, to a larger extent, consider themselves to have the relevant education (66.2%); 19.4% perceive themselves as underqualified and 14.5% as overqualified. The higher share of self-reported overqualified young workers in rural areas reinforces the idea that higher-skilled occupations are more out of reach there than in urban areas.

However, the normative skills mismatch measurement tells us quite a different story. On average, only 39.4% of rural young workers have the level of education required for their current occupation (Figure 1.15 Panel B). Bangladesh and Uganda are extreme cases: 74.0% and 55.4% of rural youth think they have the relevant qualification, but in reality 91.3% and 94.5%, respectively, are underqualified. Skills mismatch in developing countries is essentially a problem of underqualification, i.e. individuals have not completed the level of education that is, in principle, required in their occupational group. While 17.9% of rural young workers are affected by overqualification, which is already quite significant, no less than 42.7% are underqualified. Underqualification is thus a major issue for youth in rural areas. Skills mismatch and, in particular, underqualification, is less pervasive in urban areas, stressing again the greater need for more productive and skilled jobs in rural settings. In fact, 46.9% of urban young workers have completed the level of education required for their current occupation, 35.6% are underqualified and 17.4% are overqualified. Underqualification of rural youth is more prevalent in sub-Saharan African countries and in Asian countries. In addition to Bangladesh and Uganda, the share of underqualified rural young workers also reaches extremes in Liberia (81.4%), Malawi (83.2%) and Bangladesh (91.3%).

Figure 1.15. Rural young workers' skills mismatch using subjective and normative measures

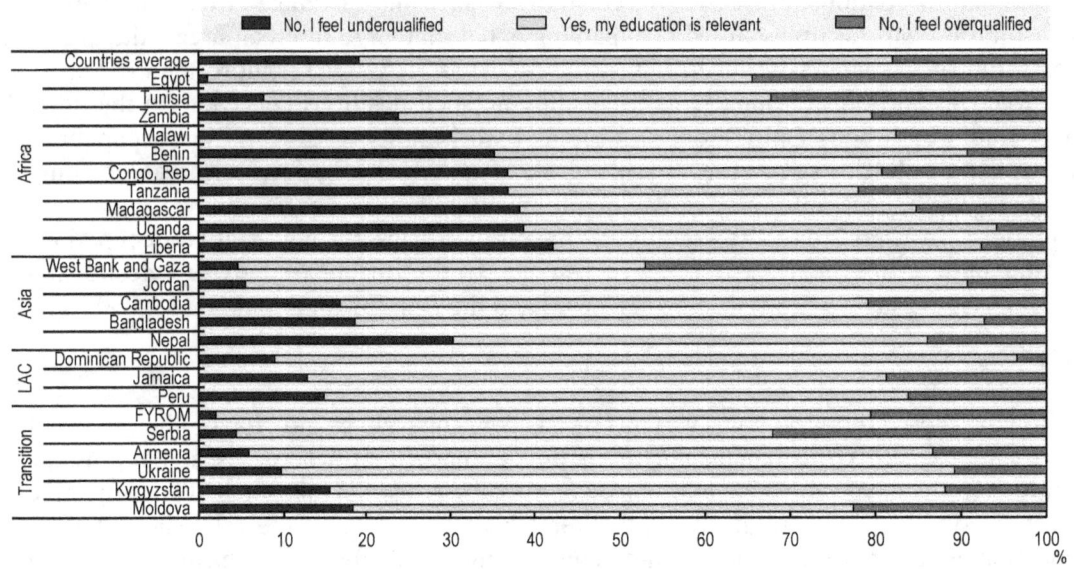

Panel A. Rural young workers' perceptions about the relevance of their education to their current job requirements

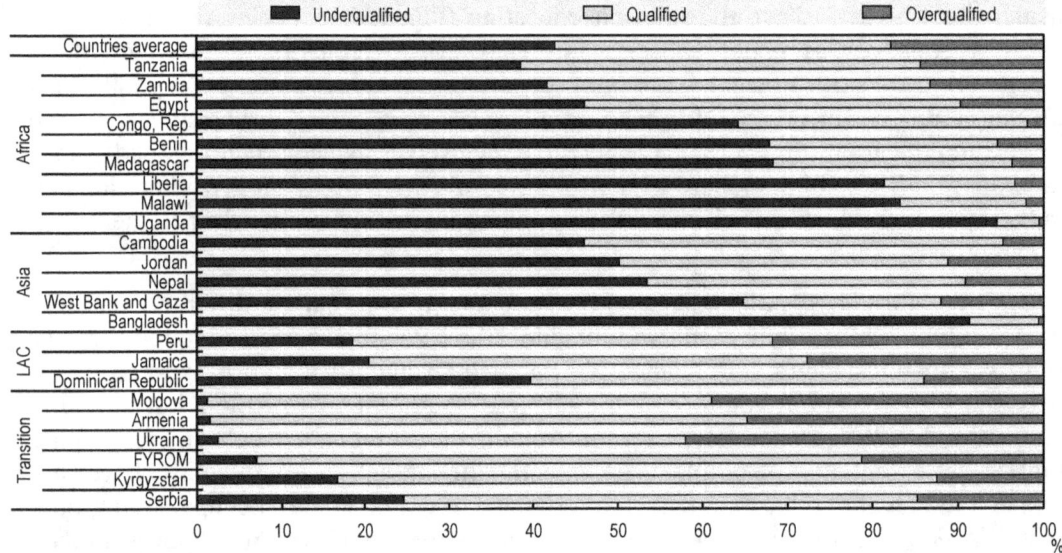

Panel B. Qualification according to a normative mismatch measure based on the level of education required for each type of occupation

1. See Notes 1-4 of Figure 1.2.
2. The normative mismatch measure is based on a mapping of ISCO-08 major groups to ISCED skills levels as follows: An individual working in a high-skilled occupation (ISCO 1-3) should have completed at least some tertiary education, an individual working in a medium-skilled occupation (ISCO 4-8) should have completed (general or vocational) secondary education and an individual working in a low-skilled occupation (ISCO 9) should have completed at least primary education. These individuals are considered adequately qualified and, if not, they enter into the over- or underqualified category.
3. Panel B data are missing for Tunisia.

Source: Authors' own calculations based on ILO's School-to-Work Transition Survey data from 2012 to 2015.

Not all sectors of activity are equally affected by skills mismatch in rural areas. Skills mismatch and underqualification are most prevalent in the agricultural sector, with only

33.2% of rural young workers having the relevant qualification, while 51.2% are underqualified (Figure 1.16).

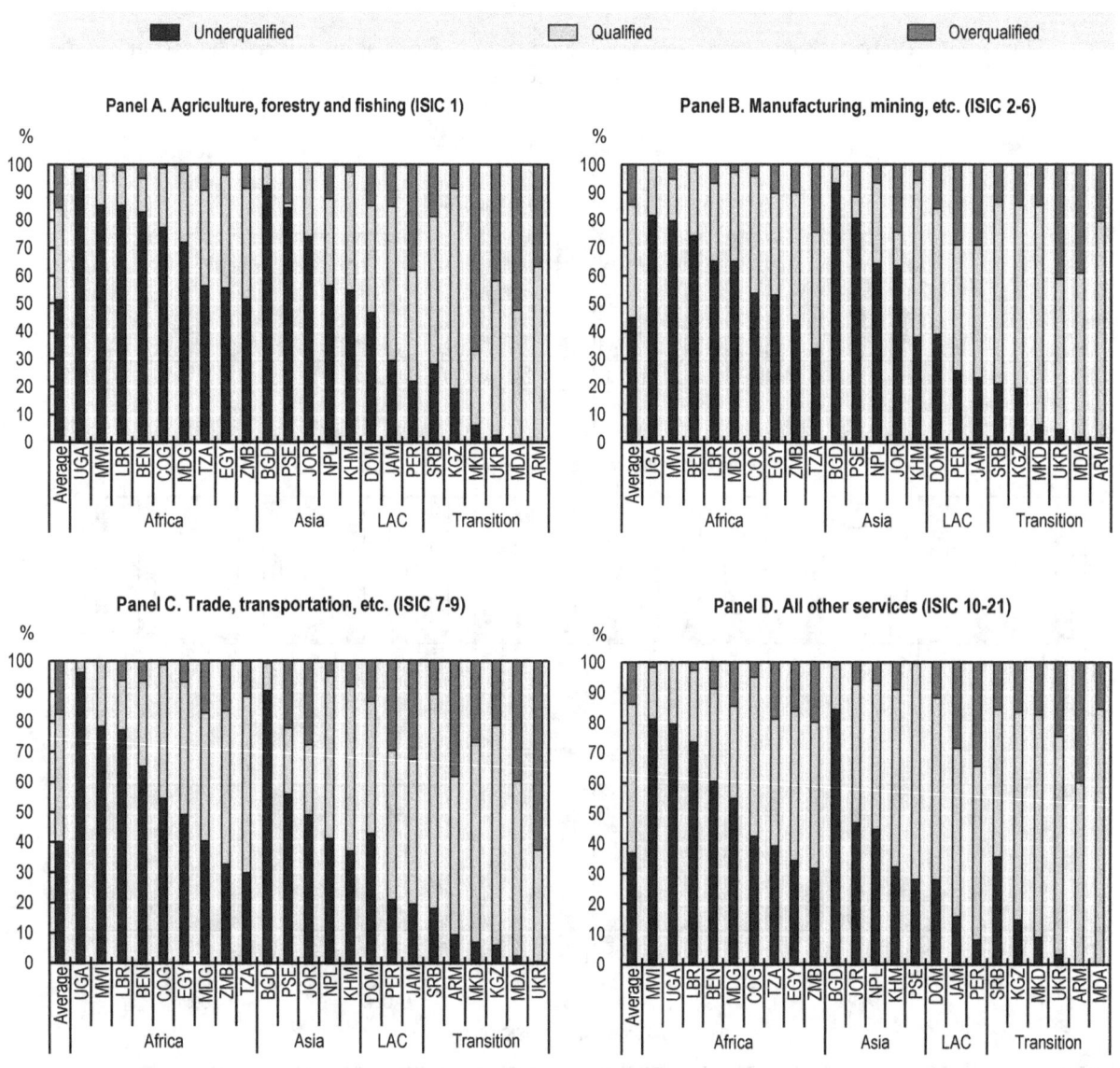

Figure 1.16. Distribution of rural young workers by normative skills mismatch category and sector of activity, %

1. See Notes 1-2 of Figure 1.15.
2. Data are missing for Tunisia.
Source: Authors' own calculations based on ILO's School-to-Work Transition Survey data from 2012 to 2015.

Overqualification is, on the other hand, quite marginal at 15.5%. While skills mismatch in the agricultural sector is a widespread phenomenon in rural areas, in the other sectors things are better. Among rural young workers in manufacturing, 40.8% are likely to have the relevant qualifications, while in trade and transportation this share is 42.2%, and in all other services this share is 49.4%. Less than half – 44.8%, 40.1% and 36.8%, respectively – are underqualified in these sectors. Compared with agriculture, skills mismatch and underqualification in all other sectors is less of a problem, whereas overqualification is becoming one in trade and transportation (17.7%). In most of the African and Asian countries surveyed, the vast majority of rural young workers engaged in agricultural activities are underqualified. Furthermore, it is also in the agriculture sector that, overall, rural young workers perceive themselves as the most underqualified (subjective measure) by comparison with other sectors (Figure 1.17).

Figure 1.17. Distribution of rural young workers by subjective skills mismatch category and sector of activity, %

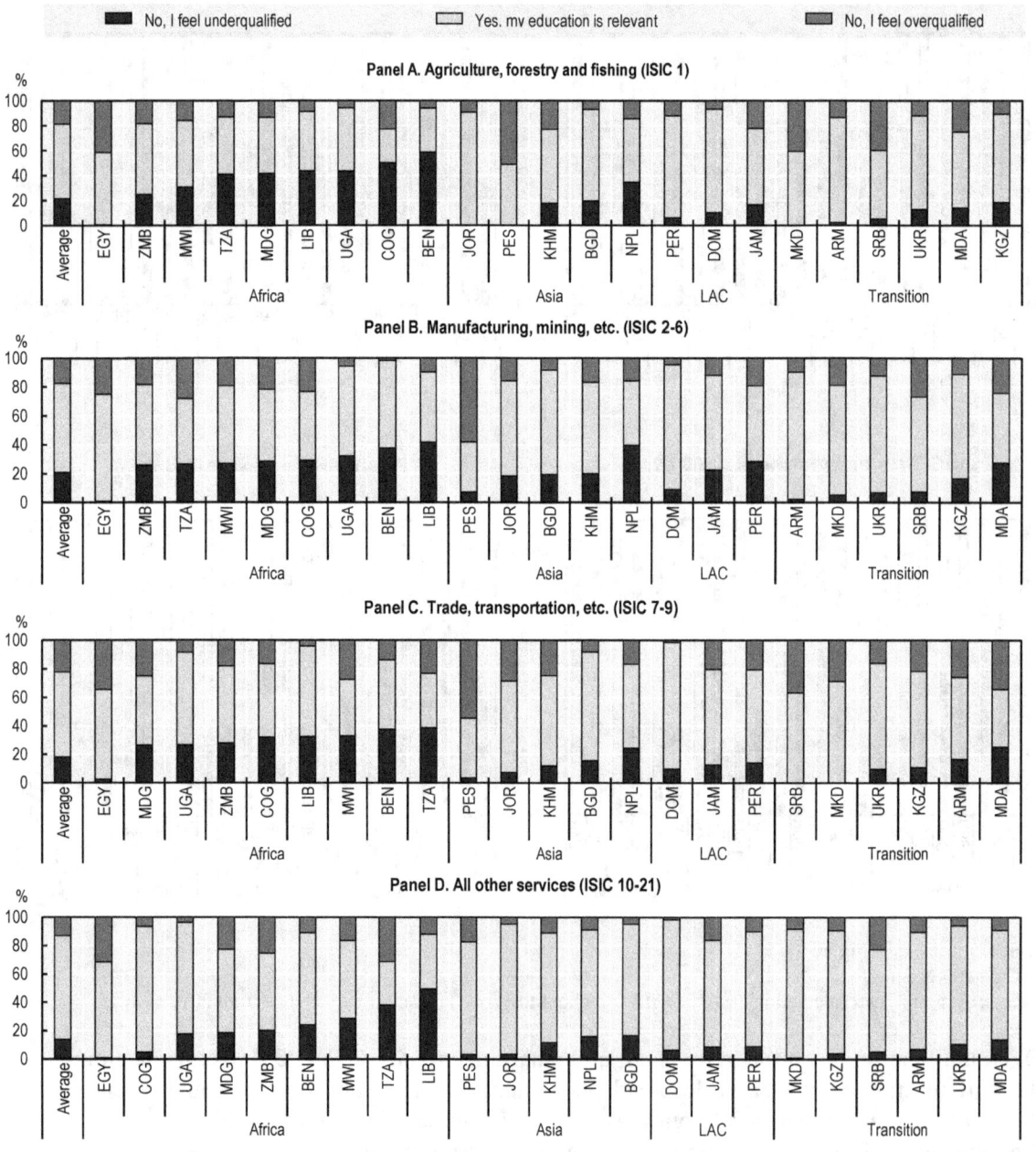

1. See Note 1 of Figure 1.15.
2. Data are missing for Tunisia.
Source: Authors' own calculations based on ILO's School-to-Work Transition Survey data from 2012 to 2015.

Conclusion

The global youth population today is at its highest ever, with one in six persons in the world aged between 15 and 24. The highest proportion of youth today lives in Africa and Asia. In Africa, the youth population will continue to increase until 2050. Although large disparities are observed across countries, the majority of youth in developing countries still live in rural areas. Rural young people are a socially and spatially diverse group and several factors will influence their employment outcomes, including their level of education and skills, gender, location, social norms, social networks, and access to assets such as land, finance and knowledge.

Educational attainment among rural youth in developing countries is generally low and large numbers work in vulnerable jobs and agricultural activities. One in five rural youth never attended school and barely half have at best completed primary education. Agriculture remains the main provider of jobs for rural youth, but the sector is characterised in developing countries by low productivity and earnings and poor working conditions. This results in very few rural youth having high-skilled positions. Self-employment and contribution to family work, usually considered vulnerable jobs, are dominant forms of employment. Wage employment constitutes a less important share of rural youth employment, except in Asia-Pacific, where manufacturing has been expanding along with urbanisation trends.

It is no surprise that rural youth aspire to more and better. They want better pay, more stable jobs, greater social status and improved working and living conditions. In fact, the majority of rural youth currently studying want to be in high-skilled occupations, but in reality, few will end up doing as they wish. High levels of aspirations can only fuel frustration when skills mismatch is a real problem and labour demand in rural areas remains low. In rural areas, skills mismatch and underqualification are most pervasive in the agricultural sector. Moreover, a persistent high level of job dissatisfaction among youth in agriculture fosters rural outmigration. Narrowing these gaps, both in aspirations and in skills mismatch, will require both supply-side and demand-side policy actions.

Notes

[1] Although the 24 SWTS countries are clearly not representative of the global youth population, they nonetheless mirror the diversity of the developing world in terms of both geographical location and income level. Based on the 2018 World Bank country income classifications, we have 7 countries classified as low-income economies (Benin, Liberia, Madagascar, Malawi, Nepal, Tanzania and Uganda); 12 as lower-middle income economies (Armenia, Bangladesh, Cambodia, Congo (Republic of the), Egypt, Jordan, Kyrgyzstan, Moldova, Tunisia, Ukraine, West Bank and Gaza, and Zambia); and 5 as upper middle-income economies (Dominican Republic, FYROM, Jamaica, Peru and Serbia). In terms of geographical location, 8 countries are located in sub-Saharan Africa (Benin, Liberia, Madagascar, Malawi, Tanzania, Uganda, Congo (Republic of the) and Zambia), 6 in Europe and Central Asia (Armenia, FYROM, Kyrgyzstan, Moldova, Serbia and Ukraine), 4 in the Middle East and North Africa (Egypt, Jordan, Tunisia, and West Bank and Gaza), 3 in Latin America and the Caribbean (Dominican Republic, Jamaica and Peru), 2 in South Asia (Bangladesh and Nepal), and 1 in East Asia and the Pacific (Cambodia). For the sake of readability, countries are divided in all the graphs of this chapter into four broad regions: Africa, Asia, Latin America and the Caribbean, and Transition countries.

[2] Note that some countries have joined a higher income group since the year of the survey (e.g. Bangladesh, Cambodia, Peru).

[3] The only low-income economies not in sub-Saharan Africa are Afghanistan, Democratic People's Republic of Korea, Haiti and Nepal.

[4] Vulnerable employment refers to own-account workers and contributing family workers.

[5] Mining and quarrying are often mistakenly included in the secondary sector; however, this should not be the case because these are extractive activities and therefore relate to primary production.

References

Elder, S. et al. (2015), "Youth and rural development: Evidence from 25 school-to-work transition surveys", *Work4Youth Publication Series* No. 29, International Labour Office, Geneva.

FAO (2016), *Migration, Agriculture and Rural Development: Addressing the Root Causes of Migration and Harnessing its Potential for Development*, Food and Agriculture Organization of the United Nations, Rome.

FAO (2015), "Reducing distress migration through decent rural employment", *Rural Transformations – Information Note No. 4*, Food and Agriculture Organization of the United Nations, Rome.

FAO (2010), "Making migration work for women and men in rural labour markets", *Gender and Rural Employment Policy Brief No. 6*, Food and Agriculture Organization of the United Nations, Rome.

FAO (1991), "Rural Youth Situation, Needs and Prospects - An overview with special emphasis on Africa", a paper presented at the sub-regional workshop on population and rural youth, Nairobi, Kenya, Food and Agriculture Organization of the United Nations, Rome.

ILO (n.d.), "Inventory of official national-level statistical definitions for rural/urban areas", International Labour Organization, http://www.ilo.org/wcmsp5/groups/public/---dgreports/---stat/documents/genericdocument/wcms_389373.pdf (accessed December 2017)

ILO (2015), *Asia-Pacific Labour Market Update: October 2015*, ILO Regional Office for Asia and the Pacific, Bangkok.

ILO (2012a), *Global Employment Trends 2012: Preventing a Deeper Jobs Crisis*, International Labour Office, Geneva.

ILO (2012b), *International Standard Classification of Occupations (ISCO-08), Volume 1: Structure, Group Definitions and Correspondence Tables*, International Labour Organization, Geneva.

ILO (1993), "Resolution concerning the International Classification of Status in Employment (ICSE), adopted by the Fifteenth International Conference of Labour Statisticians", International Labour Organization, http://www.ilo.org/wcmsp5/groups/public/---dgreports/---stat/documents/normativeinstrument/wcms_087562.pdf.

OECD (2017), *Youth Aspirations and the Reality of Jobs in Developing Countries: Mind the Gap*, Development Centre Studies, OECD Publishing, Paris, http://dx.doi.org/10.1787/9789264285668-en.

OECD Development Centre (2014), *Social Institutions and Gender Index Synthesis Report*, OECD, Paris.

Sumberg, J. et al. (2014), "Young people, agriculture, and employment in rural Africa", *WIDER Working Paper 2014/080*, World Institute for Development Economics Research, United Nations University, Helsinki, Finland.

UNDESA (2017), *World Population Prospects: The 2017 Revision*, United Nations, Department of Economic and Social Affairs, Population Division, New York.

UNDESA (2015), *World Urbanization Prospects: The 2014 Revision*, United Nations, Department of Economic and Social Affairs, Population Division, New York.

UNESCAP (2016), *Economic and Social Survey of Asia and the Pacific 2015: Year-end Update*, United Nations Economic and Social Commission for Asia and the Pacific, Bangkok.

UNFPA (2014), *State of World Population 2014: The Power of 1.8 Billion*, United Nations Population Fund, New York.

UNSD (n.d.), "Population density and urbanization", https://unstats.un.org/unsd/demographic/sconcerns/densurb/densurbmethods.htm#B (accessed December 2017).

World Bank (2014), "Report on the remittance agenda of the G20", prepared by the World Bank for the G20 Australian Presidency, Washington, DC.

World Bank/IFAD (2017), "Rural youth employment", paper commissioned by the German Federal Ministry for Economic Cooperation and Development as Input Document for the G20 - Development Working Group.

Chapter 2. Approaches for youth inclusion along the agricultural value chain

Growth in demand for value-added food and processed agricultural products in developing countries is an opportunity to develop the agro-industries for youth employment creation. However, challenges remain in enabling small-scale farmers and low-skilled rural youth to integrate into local and global agricultural value chains and move up the ladder to meet the quantity and quality standards required for both national and export markets. Examples in this chapter describe different interventions at the local level that can help integrate rural youth into the agricultural value chain and provide them with employment opportunities. It draws success factors for integrating youth into agricultural value chains using a youth employment lens.

Faced with the daunting youth employment challenge, governments are increasingly promoting youth entrepreneurship as a way to expand employment and earning opportunities. Success stories of young agripreneurs and entrepreneurs in agribusinesses are numerous and become a source of inspiration for other young people (see Box 2.1). Few young people will become successful entrepreneurs, however. Recent work by the Organisation for Economic Co-operation and Development (OECD) on youth entrepreneurship in Côte d'Ivoire, Madagascar, Peru and Viet Nam finds that successful entrepreneurs represent only a tiny proportion of youth entrepreneurs and usually have specific educational profiles, personal characteristics and endowments that the majority of youth in developing countries do not have (OECD, 2017). The vast majority are confined to subsistence and informal activities, and for many in rural areas, to low-paid jobs in agriculture. These findings cast doubts on how much hope policy makers can place on youth entrepreneurship as a solution to the growing youth employment challenge, especially in rural areas where physical operating conditions are poor and where the vast majority of youth are low skilled.

The potential for creating quality jobs for rural youth exists, however. Investing and building capabilities in agri-food industries (production, processing, preservation and other handling processes, as well as packaging and marketing) indeed remain largely underexploited. Domestic demand for diversified foods is rising in many developing countries and agricultural value chain development presents a real opportunity to support local enterprises and improve market structures and business environments that can result in more entrepreneurs as well as wage jobs. In West Africa, a study estimates that the food economy, which includes producing food and retailing food to consumers, already accounts for 66% of total employment (64% of working youth aged 20-29), 82 million jobs and 35% of regional gross domestic product (GDP) (Allen and Heinrigs, 2016). The majority (78%) of these jobs are in the low end of the value chain, mostly in agricultural production. When using full-time equivalents, the share of agriculture in total food economy employment drops to 68%. Off-farm jobs downstream in the value chain, e.g. in processing and services, constitute a minor share of employment opportunities (Allen, Heinrigs and Heo, 2018). However, given the size of the food economy, these activities play an important role in overall employment, accounting for 31% of total non-farm jobs in the region.

Agriculture remains the main employment sector in rural areas and for youth. Youth Well-being Policy Reviews carried out in nine developing countries found high rates of youth employment in agriculture in Cambodia (50%), Côte d'Ivoire (44%), Malawi (58%), and Viet Nam (33%) (OECD Development Centre, 2018, 2017a, 2017b and 2017c). These shares are even higher among rural youth (Figure 1.4). In sub-Saharan Africa, the overall share of youth employment in agriculture is highest in low- and low-middle-income countries where the majority of youth are low skilled and low educated. The agricultural labour force is expected to continue to grow in Africa and decrease in developing Asia (Table 2.1).

Table 2.1. Total agricultural labour force 2016-20

	2016	2017	2018	2019	2020
Developing Africa ('000)	246 969	252 167	257 443	262 791	268 220
Developing Asia ('000)	1 020 286	1 017 531	1 013 914	1 009 605	1 004 753

Source: UNCTAD statistics, http://unctadstat.unctad.org/wds/TableViewer/tableView.aspx.

This chapter analyses ten initiatives specifically intended to create youth employment along agri-food value chains, especially for disadvantaged rural youth and draws on the key success factors for integrating youth into agri-food value chains. Most of the projects target youth with primary or secondary education levels. The review also found more examples in agricultural production and much less in processing and other downstream activities. All initiatives intend to combine local market opportunities and skills development for youth.

Agricultural production provides an entry point for low-skilled rural youth to engage in the agri-food value chain

An integrated public-private partnership model for youth employment in agriculture, Tanzania

Beneficiaries' profile: 18-35 year-old women and men, out of school with primary or secondary education

Number of youth beneficiaries: 400 trained as facilitators with a spillover effect of, on average, 1:20, i.e. 7 600 in total

In Tanzania, agriculture is the mainstay of the economy, employing 80% of the working population and accounting for 64% of all exports. The service sector, which has been growing rapidly in recent years, accounts for approximately 47% of GDP. Economic growth has not been able to generate adequate employment to absorb increases in the labour force and reduce the proportion of the unemployed and underemployed (FAO, 2014).

Since 2011, the Food and Agriculture Organization (FAO) has developed an innovative public-private partnership model for youth employment in agriculture and has piloted the model in Malawi, Tanzania Mainland and Zanzibar archipelago. The focus was on rural-based young farmers, who were out of school, with primary and/or secondary education. Most of the youth engaged in the project (60%) reported using their families' land, while the rest rented it.

The approach

A central component of the model is the strengthening of human capital, with knowledge and information adapted to rural contexts, labour demand and viable economic opportunities, and the level of youth understanding. The model uses Junior Farmer Field and Life Schools (JFFLS), which provide vocational training specifically tailored to rural settings, combined with employment promotion and access to markets. It is specifically tailored for teaching children and young people about agricultural, business and life skills and encouraging self-organisation. The specific training areas are chosen together with the youth in collaboration with the partners, and on the basis of the local needs and opportunities.

The private sector (in this case, co-operatives) plays an important role in shaping the food and agriculture systems, influencing entrepreneurs to engage in more production and service provision, and providing an enabling working environment. With this in mind, the model introduces a public-private partnership approach to facilitate youth access to assets (land, financial services, technology) and agricultural sector markets. FAO developed a set of criteria to select potential private sector partners (Table 2.2).

Table 2.2. **Criteria to select potential private-sector partners**

Criteria	Precondition	Added value
Conformity to FAO's mandate and work programme	X	
Ethical values in the major sustainable business model principles of honesty, openness, transparency, sustainability (economic and environmental), democracy, social responsibility, inclusiveness, equality and solidarity	X	
Mutual interests and objectives	X	
Demonstrated activeness in protecting smallholders' rights	X	
Access to land, credit and markets services	X	
Country-wide coverage		X
Long-standing presence in the country		X
Involvement on behalf of the private sector and smallholder farmers in the implementation of the Comprehensive Africa Agriculture Development Programme (CAADP)		X

Source: FAO (2014), "FAO, private and public partnership model for youth employment in agriculture: Experiences from Malawi, Tanzania Mainland and Zanzibar archipelago".

In Tanzania, the project collaborated with the Tanzania Federation of Cooperatives, a national co-operative umbrella organisation comprising 6 000 co-operative societies, including specialised savings and credit unions with approximately 700 000 members. Land has been provided in certain cases by producers' organisations (through co-operative land) or by regional authorities (through village land). Linkages with the co-operative unions (savings and credit co-operatives, SACCOs) and dedicated agricultural budgets from regional authorities facilitated youth access to finance.

Producers' organisations played an important role in guiding and supporting the youth groups in their choice of potential agricultural activities and products' placement in the market at fairly negotiated prices. The private sector included the National Smallholder Farmers' Association of Malawi, the Tanzania Federation of Cooperatives and the Cooperative Union of Zanzibar. In parallel, strong efforts have been channelled towards public partnerships in order to sustainably integrate the activities into national strategies and programmes, e.g. by supporting the development of a National Strategy for Youth Involvement in Agriculture in Tanzania.

Across Tanzania, both young women and men had a strong preference for crop production, with maize, groundnuts, soya and soya beans being the most cultivated crops. Livestock rearing represented a less commonly chosen activity, and other activities such as fishing represented a rather limited share. Youth have primarily sold their products with a small profit margin (about 20%), with a majority of them expressing a desire to start adding value in order to improve their economic opportunities.

Results

The training of youth facilitators (farmers themselves) had an important spillover effect on peer-to-peer learning in their communities. The youth facilitators are trained by master trainers from the government, who are themselves trained to train youth. Youth facilitators were able to mobilise and sensitise their peers regarding opportunities offered by the agricultural sector. On average, each facilitator retrains 20 other rural youth in his/her district. In Tanzania, one FAO-trained youth was able to mobilise and train 150 peers in his home district, create a group and secure 300 acres of government land from the Regional Commission to start up their commercial activities.

During assessments conducted after the training at regular intervals of six months, youth reported an increase in economic returns of approximately 60% by farming their 1-5 acres (0.4 to 2 hectares) of land and adopting new practices learnt during the training. The number of young people engaged in the sector increased, as did their memberships of local producers' organisations, co-operatives and unions. Trained youth have returned to their communities with renewed enthusiasm and have both created awareness and trained their peers, displaying a positive shift in the perception of agriculture by comparison with other non-trained youth. They perceive agriculture not just from a commercial perspective, but also one that is environmental friendly. Finally, the government developed a strategy to guide all stakeholders interested in youth employment, with the Ministry of Agriculture responsible for co-ordinating the design and implementation of programmes.

In the framework of the current United Nations Joint Programme on Youth Employment for Tanzania, a recent study was undertaken to identify the sectors that might have the highest potential to create opportunities for youth employment and that were more appealing to youth. Initial results show that horticulture, apiculture, oil seeds and tourism linked to agriculture seem to be the most appealing sectors to youth (UN, 2016).

Success factors

- **Partnerships:** Establishing partnerships with governments and private sector actors has been key to fostering an enabling environment for youth employment and youth inclusion in national and regional initiatives; the private sector partners selected have proven to be pivotal in the institutionalisation of the model, and thus its sustainability.

- **Capacity development:** The training component was key to attracting young people to engage in agriculture. The facilitation and training delivered were crucial. Large-scale impacts were achieved through spillover effects created by the youth themselves when returning to their villages, rather than with the selective youth trained directly by FAO. In addition, peer training is a way to empower young people by giving them the opportunity to participate in interactive experiential learning and then share this knowledge with their peers in their community.

Local youth associations and family farm advisors to support local food production, Senegal

Beneficiaries' profiles: Unemployed young people aged 18-30, from vulnerable households

Number of youth beneficiaries: 13 115 (8 170 female, 4 945 male)

In Senegal, 55% of the population lives in rural areas. A recent study by the National Statistical Agency revealed that 48.5% of the labour force was in the primary sector (agriculture, livestock and fishery) while 26.3% and 12.1% were in the service and industry sectors, respectively. Indeed, the youth labour force is largely unskilled, with the majority engaged in agricultural activities (Hathie, 2014). Migration appears to be a popular alternative for many young Senegalese faced with unemployment or underemployment. Young people are migrating internally but also to other countries, mainly to other African countries, followed by European countries. Data from the World Bank's "African migration survey 2010" show that the average age of Senegalese migrants (rural-rural, rural-urban) was 32, with 54% being men and 45% being women (Shimeles, 2010). Poverty, climate change, deterioration of the environment, conflicts and lack of infrastructure in rural areas are some of the main reasons for migrating.

In Senegal's groundnut basin, the youth population represents over 60% of the total population. The International Fund for Agricultural Development (IFAD)-supported Agricultural Value Chains Development Project (Projet d'appui aux filières agricoles [PAFA]) aims to improve the incomes and livelihoods of poor farm families in that geographic area, with a special focus on turning farming into a thriving business for young people. One of the target groups of the programme is underemployed young people aged 18-30 years.

The project focuses on the consolidation of profitable value chains based on the local agroecological potential. The project promotes the use of local products, such as millet/sorghum, maize, bissap/hibiscus, sesame, niebe, rice, poultry, and market gardening (onions, tomatoes, carrots, cabbage). Off-farm employment was generated in agricultural extension activities (the youth counselling within each producer organisation), processing (e.g. decorticating rice) and transforming (mostly women cooking).

The approach

PAFA has been using an innovative targeting approach to create jobs for rural youth. The project encouraged local sports and cultural associations to prepare proposals. Youth were mostly self-employed and could participate through mixed groups or youth-only groups (associations sportives et culturelles [ASC]). The youth groups prepared proposals and benefited from a series of services, including equipment, training on best agricultural practices and improved inputs. Some young people already had access to land, but many had to negotiate with their families with the support of their ASC, young agricultural extension officers, and mixed-age farmer groups.

The project targeted farmers' organisations as main project holders, and youth and women as sub-project holders ("porteurs de sous-projets").[1] This meant that the farmers' organisations themselves had an interest in helping young people gain access to land. For market gardening, access to land (along with certified seeds and fertilisers) was guaranteed by the fact that the land to which the project provided irrigation was assigned from the start to youth and women. This was generally community land that was granted to youth and women's groups by the village authorities and set up for gardening by the project.

The project provided subsidies to acquire quality inputs (certified seeds, fertilisers and agricultural equipment) by setting up a system of "in-kind savings" (e.g. storage of agricultural produce). The subsidies decreased over three years (from 80% to 40%). This system ensured farmers' access to quality inputs, empowered organisations to access inputs and strengthened their capacity to mobilise savings of beneficiary households.

A number of farmers (1 096 women under 35 years old) were trained as "family farm advisors" to inform farmers on good practices in family poultry production. In addition, over 800 women and young girls were trained in processing and cooking techniques using local cereals, in order to promote the consumption of local products. Hotel and restaurant owners have been encouraged to introduce dishes prepared with local products in their menus.

Finally, the project supported the groups to access market information and to identify and sign contracts with market operators. National agents for inter-professional organisations (les cadres nationaux d'interprofession filières) provided information on prices in reference markets, including through mobile SMS messages sent to farmers. The project facilitated contracts between farmers' organisations and market operators to ensure a fair negotiation and secure prices for the producers. Farmers' organisations identified and approached a market operator (a private trader, a larger farmers' organisation grouping together multiple smaller farmers' organisations, or a processor). Market operators in the region had been informed about the project through an awareness campaign that included a series of meetings. For farmers' organisations facing difficulties in identifying a market operator, the project facilitated these linkages. Once the farmers' organisation-market operator couples were formed, the project facilitated contract signings and their implementation during the first year. PAFA places emphasis on supporting these "couples" rather than on individual farmers' organisations or market operators; the farmers' organisation itself has no contract with the farmers participating in the contract-farming scheme, but regularly buys their produce if the quality is met.

In addition, youth were engaged in value chain roundtables (millet/sorghum, cowpea, sesame and hibiscus) set up by the project to bring together key value chain actors and create a dialogue around issues such as increased seed production, dissemination of information on market prices and rainfall, commercial intermediation and dispute resolution between producers and buyers, and the establishment of an internal quality control system.

Results

In total, the project assisted 45 youth associations with financial support, capacity building and access to quality inputs and equipment. As a result, almost 5 000 young men and more than 8 000 young women are now involved in agricultural value chains and have increased their income. Products of market gardening were mainly for local markets, with some youth groups negotiating with traders from Dakar. The project supported the creation of small-scale rice mill businesses managed by youth groups, which created employment for 56 young men.

Table 2.3. IFAD-supported PAFA's beneficiaries by value chain

Value chain	No. of beneficiaries	No. of women	No. of men	Youth		Adults		% of women	% of youth
				Female	Male	Female	Male		
Millet/sorghum	13 078	6 869	6 209	2 198	2 049	4 671	4 160	53%	32%
Sesame	5 837	2 667	3 170	1 040	1 046	1 627	2 124	46%	36%
Niebe	2 896	2 347	549	845	192	1 502	357	81%	36%
Bissap	4 260	3 881	380	1 281	156	2 600	224	91%	34%
Poultry	1 966	1 809	157	977	102	832	55	92%	55%
Rice	3 500	2 135	1 365	598	478	1 537	887	61%	31%
Rice mill	56		56	0	56	0	0	0%	100%
Market gardening	1 085	674	412	235	144	437	268	62%	35%
Maize and others	5 056	2 932	2 124	997	722	1 935	1 402	58%	34%
Total	37 736	23 314	14 422	8 171	4 945	15 141	9 477	62%	35%

Source: IFAD (2016b), Projet d'Appui aux Filières Agricoles (PAFA), Rapport de supervision, Département gestion des programmes.

In addition, young farmers have shown an increasing enthusiasm for farming, and rural outmigration in villages supported by the project has reduced. Beyond the direct beneficiaries, the project also attracted young graduates, who decided to return to their villages and engage in farming as a business. Beyond the group of targeted vulnerable youth, several youths studying at the university in Dakar started farming activities in their villages in the value chains promoted by the project (e.g. sesame production). As members of the producer organisations, they benefited from agricultural extension services supported by the project.

Success factors

- **Building on existing institutions:** Some young people indicated they preferred being in youth sport and cultural associations rather than in a mixed age group where they had no voice.

- **Awareness campaigns:** Raising awareness among youth about the opportunity of agriculture as a profitable business and as an income generator comparable to wages in the city helped mobilise youth participation. This awareness campaign was initially carried out by the project, but during the course of implementation the ASC supported by the project started conducting awareness activities themselves among youth. In fact, young farmers informed other young people about the benefits of their new farming activities (e.g. sesame production), giving incentives for their friends who had left for the city to come back to rural areas.

- **Peer-to-peer learning:** Agricultural extension services carried out by youth ("family farm advisers") seem particularly helpful for spreading best agricultural practices among young farmers, while perhaps less effective when reaching out to older farmers.

Individual mentorship through local volunteers, youth associations and professionals, Mali

Beneficiaries' profiles: Uneducated or undereducated rural out-of-school youth, aged 14-25

Number of youth beneficiaries: 10 489

Mali continues to have a predominantly young population, with an average age of 14 years. The effects of conflicts and food crises have aggravated the country's high rate of youth unemployment and underemployment. The Mali Out-of-School Youth project (USAID, 2015), supported by the US Agency for International Development (USAID), was implemented in the region of Timbuktu in Mali between 2011 and 2015. The project targeted youth within the 14-25 years age group. Prior to launching the first cohort in the south, a market opportunity study was conducted for the southern regions to identify promising livelihood possibilities and local value chains for rural youth. Based on this study, youth were trained in a diverse range of agricultural activities: market gardening, grain cultivation, livestock fattening, poultry raising and the transformation of agricultural products. Other technical training included the production and repair of agricultural equipment and material, soap making, establishing a small restaurant or bakery, carpentry, masonry, sewing, hairdressing, photography, and mobile phone repair.

The approach

The project's model focused primarily on the promotion of self-employment of uneducated youth, and included basic education and entrepreneurship skills development. Youth volunteers and unemployed university or professional school graduates were in charge of dispensing the basic education and entrepreneurship courses. Each participant received a mobile phone with a preloaded learning application, including the curricular content in support of the literacy, numeracy, functional French and entrepreneurship courses. This provided youth with the opportunity to review course work outside of class in a systematic manner. Beyond these courses, youth volunteers took on mentorship roles to accompany the youth in starting their economic activities. This was done in collaboration with the youth associations.

For each activity, the project identified local professionals living in reasonable proximity to the youth to serve as trainers, so that training could be provided at the village level and to facilitate post-training follow-up visits by the trainers to each youth individually. Trainers worked with a maximum of 20 youth per site, and training focused on practical application of the content. Each trainer was given a stipend to purchase the basic supplies needed for practical demonstrations during training.

Under the project model, youth associations were selected in each village to support the volunteers and overall project implementation. Youth association members played a key role in monitoring youth participation in basic education classes, technical training and other activities. When attendance problems arose, representatives from the youth association immediately visited the family to understand the reasons for the absence and encourage parents and the youth to continue the training.

Once they completed their training, the participants received a starter kit with the minimum set of equipment and material needed to launch their microenterprise. In addition, a total of 9 534 youth (including 5 802 women) participated in the savings and internal lending community groups that the project helped support. Members committed to saving a specific sum each month and learned the principles of saving and lending, charging small amounts of interest on loans, and delivering penalties for late payments. Each community group established two funds: a general fund that provided loans for microenterprise development and a social fund that provided loans for personal needs such as illnesses, marriages and baptisms. The average loan value of loans for productive activities was USD 14, a relatively small sum that often made the difference in a youth's ability to develop his or her microenterprise (for example, to buy needed ingredients/raw materials or to transport his or her goods to a nearby market). Women took out over 65% of the loans. When appropriate, youth were introduced to microfinance institutions within their region.

Results

Seventy-three percent (8 077) of the youth who completed the training started their microenterprise, either individually or in groups. As of November 2015, 70% of youth who launched microenterprises between 2011 and 2013 were still operating their businesses. Of those youth still operating a microenterprise, 64% were self-employed, while the rest were managing their microenterprises with their families. Women tended to run their businesses as self-employed individuals, whereas men were more likely to run their businesses with their families. In addition, about 85% of the youth had experienced an increase in profits since they had launched their microenterprises. Women, in particular, were more likely than men to have maintained their income-generating activities.

Success factors

- **Mentorship:** Local volunteer leaders and youth associations facilitated youth participation in the project, raising awareness among families and engaging youth in community services.

- **Proximity of training:** Providing skills training directly to youth in their villages through local trainers, rather than sending youth to training centres in larger towns or cities far from the villages, helped trainees maintain regular attendance.

- **Starter kits:** The distribution of income-generating activity starter kits and the project's savings and internal lending communities positively contributed to helping youth launch their microenterprises after the training.

Limitations

- **Absence of childcare facilities:** The majority of women were already married with 2-3 young children. The competing priorities of participating in courses and providing for their families were stressful and often contributed to irregular attendance among young women. Arrangements should be made to provide childcare for those with small children so that they are better able to concentrate in class and benefit from the courses.

- **Need to differentiate age groups:** The age range of the project participants was 14-25; however, younger adolescents (14-17) differ in significant ways from older youth and typically would need a differentiated curriculum, which the project was unable to provide. The project recommended raising the recruitment age to a minimum of 17 years rather than 14 years. In the case of a project intending to maintain the broader age range, the youth should be divided into younger and older groups and a new curriculum developed for the younger group, designed to better respond to their needs.

Pathways to sustainable rural livelihoods, Burkina Faso, Egypt, Ethiopia, Malawi and Uganda

Beneficiaries' profiles: Rural, out-of-school youth aged 12-18

Number of youth beneficiaries: 3 849

Launched in 2012, Youth in Action is a six-year learning and livelihoods programme implemented by Save the Children in partnership with the MasterCard Foundation. The programme seeks to improve the socio economic status of rural, out-of-school young people – girls and boys aged 12-18 – in Burkina Faso, Egypt, Ethiopia, Malawi and Uganda.

The approach

Youth in Action is structured in a way that encourages youth to make their own decisions. It provides a three-pronged approach to its programming: learning for life, taking action, and mentorship and aftercare.

The approach supports youth to identify and explore agriculture-related livelihood opportunities through a combination of informal educational and practice-oriented learning experiences. The youth cohort go through a minimum of six months' training, where the first three months are centred on acquiring knowledge around literacy, numeracy, financial literacy, employability and life skills. The curriculum builds on young people's own knowledge, perspectives and experiences while encouraging them to explore their environments and learn about themselves, their families, their communities and their livelihood opportunities.

The last three months are entitled the "action phase", where youth translate their learning into sustainable livelihoods through pathways of their choice. During this phase, youth are provided with four pathway choices: education, enterprise, vocational training and apprenticeship.

- The education pathway provides youth, especially those aged between 12 and 14 years, with an opportunity to go back to formal school.
- The enterprise pathway allows youth to start up small businesses within their communities, supported by local experts.
- The vocational training pathway involves youth joining vocational training institutions, where they are formally trained in different trades around agriculture.
- The apprenticeship pathway links youth to local artisans within their communities to acquire specific skills in different trades.

Each country has adapted the approach to select the pathways relevant to its context. Each youth chooses one pathway and selects one business within that pathway. The programme then supports participants towards the pathway they selected by providing technical assistance, financial aid (small grants) assistance, networking and links to the local market, peer to peer guidance, and support before they graduate and celebrate their achievements. The programme creates partnerships with families and communities, local trade and business associations, local non-governmental organisations (NGOs), and governments to facilitate youth engagement and advocate for systematic changes.

Results

In the five countries where the project is implemented, most youth have chosen the enterprise pathway since it provides an immediate opportunity to start their own businesses. Youth usually started a business that one of their family members was engaged in.

As of March 2016, 3 849 youth have benefited from the programme, including 1 670 girls and 2 179 boys. Some 1 821 have chosen their pathway, and many youth have received apprenticeship training and toolkits related to their chosen field of training.

Success factors

- **Comprehensive second-chance education:** A pathway approach with opportunities to gain key foundational skills, such as literacy and numeracy, combined with livelihood training and life-skills-building activities.
- **Parental and community support:** Awareness-building activities with families and community leaders have proven to help younger adolescents engage in rural livelihood activities and be better supported by their families. Younger adolescents are more closely tied to their family dynamic, and often their role within the family unit defines their participation in a type of agriculture livelihood opportunity.

- **Participatory approach:** Including younger cohorts in programme design and evaluation are effective methods of proactive engagement. This could include activities such as youth mapping of livelihood opportunities with rural communities, as well as peer-to-peer mentoring of younger adolescents by older peers.

New job opportunities are emerging in agribusiness services

Changes in food consumption patterns and growth in demand for value-added food and agricultural products are creating new job opportunities in developing countries. These might include self-employment or wage jobs in agribusiness processing and packaging (dairy, fruit and vegetable processing plants, storage, etc.) or services (e.g. around mechanisation, extension services, information and communications technologies [ICTs], etc.).

This section of the report presents initiatives that created youth employment both downstream and in the broader spectrum of services that support the agri-food sector. The initiatives show different opportunity spaces around the mechanisation and modernisation of agriculture, the delivery of extension services, the role of ICTs in providing service support across the value chain, and the creation of small industries in rural areas.

Youth in co-operatives for shared mechanisation, Benin

Beneficiaries' profiles: Farmers and youth farmers

Number of youth beneficiaries: 850 farmers, with over half of them youth

The level of agriculture mechanisation is very different in Asia and Africa, and also varies between and within countries and among different crops. Progress has been more significant in Asia, especially in China and India, while countries such as Cambodia doubled their usage of tractors (UNESCAP, 2016). In sub-Saharan Africa, less than 5% of farms own a tractor, and in many countries this figure drops to less than 1%. Mechanisation diminishes the burden of work and can potentially improve the attractiveness of the farming sector for youth. While greater use of machinery will undeniably replace a certain amount of manual methods for certain crops, it can also have a positive impact on employment in certain cases by solving the lack of available labour at certain times of the year and by supporting the development of other jobs around the local production (e.g. tillers, seeders, threshers and millers), operation, repair and maintenance of machinery. Beyond its impact on productivity, mechanisation contributes to reducing the work burden and changing the image of agriculture for youth. This is the case for the tractor, which is perceived by farmers, especially young ones, as a factor of modernity that can improve their social and economic situation (Balse et al., 2015).

The approach

The co-operatives for shared mechanisation (les coopératives d'utilisation de matériel agricole [CUMAs]) in Benin are based on a model developed in France with the main objective of helping farmers access machinery in order to increase farm productivity. The idea is that farmers make a collective investment and jointly use the necessary machinery to improve agricultural production. Farmers are organised in small autonomous groups of around ten farmers per CUMA. The farmers are in charge of the co-operative's management, whereas the employees are tractor drivers or mechanics. The co-operative's small size does not require hiring a director or a manager.

In 2015, there were 102 CUMAs in Benin, bringing together 850 farmers, over half of whom were youth farmers. CUMAs are created among farmers from the same village, who are sometimes already organised as groups. Each farmer must purchase a certain number of investment shares to join a CUMA, which contributes to the equity capital needed to purchase the machines. In most cases, the membership subscription amount is calculated according to the amount of cultivated land owned by each member of the co-operative. This rule allows poor farmers with the smallest areas to have access to a tractor by participating with a lower share in the co-operative. The youngest family members are often the ones who learn how to drive a tractor and join a CUMA. Some CUMAs were formed by youth groups who sell their services to farmers to finance social activities in the village.

CUMAs provide services to their members, and to non-members for a fee. The first CUMAs were engaged in ploughing and transport. Currently, some CUMAs are also developing primary transformation activities, investing in cassava graters or palm nut oil pulping machines running on thermal energy. The increased number of local co-operatives has led to the creation of a network comprising regional and district CUMAs and eventually a national federation of CUMAs. Co-ordinators of the federation offer a range of services to promote shared machinery, including training in co-operative management, tractor driving lessons, and mechanics, as well as facilitating access to spare parts. The network also partners with agricultural schools to raise awareness among students.

Results

The introduction of mechanisation has resulted in a significant increase in cultivated crop areas on each farm. Farmers interviewed in a 2014 survey indicated that they have multiplied their cropped areas by 3.5 times since they began ploughing with CUMA tractors. This increase in production areas is especially visible in cotton and maize production. In the case of the Borgou district, the increase in maize production led the members to create a co-operative for corn; the objective was to guarantee input supply to their members, to store the production and to market quality corn. In South Benin, women organised in CUMAs are performing cassava and palm oil primary transformation activities. Members of the CUMAs also indicated an increase in their income, with impacts on children's education, health and family nutrition.

An important impact of the CUMAs on youth is their change in how youth perceive farming as a profession, which they usually consider to be tough and unprofitable. First, the tractor changes the image of farming, with less drudgery and more productivity. Being a member of a CUMA is a source of pride; it conveys a certain social prestige and improves the youth's social status. In addition, farm mechanisation has removed children from the task of driving oxen, and CUMA members are able to send their children to school. In certain cases, the tractor is also used to collect fuelwood, a task traditionally performed by rural women and girls. Some CUMAs also invest in social community projects. The mechanisation co-operatives have also induced the creation of other attractive jobs for youth in rural areas, such as tractor drivers or mechanics for agricultural machinery.

CUMAs have been recognised as successful structures to access equipment. However, expansion of the model will require support in the form of public policies and funds.

Success factors

- **Social capital:** A key success factor is that the farmers joined the co-operative for a common interest and were able to build trust and solidarity. The differentiated payment scheme according to land size also gave a strong sense of ownership and fairness.

- **Partnerships:** The French CUMA network provided technical assistance and mobilised funds to support the network. The creation of a France/Benin import-export company of machinery and spare parts, Tracto Agro Africa, with a branch in France and a branch in Benin, makes it easier for CUMAs in Benin to gain access to material.

Promoting self-employment for young women close to home, India

Beneficiaries' profiles: Young women and girls

Number of youth beneficiaries: 25 000 young women and girls

The Self Employed Women's Association (SEWA) is a trade union and member-based organisation in Gujarat, India, which runs integrated development programmes that support women and girls towards self-reliance and full employment. SEWA is active in 50 districts of 12 states in India and has over 1.75 million members. It engages with 25 000 young women and girls in rural and urban areas to build their self-confidence, leadership and capacity to become thriving, self-employed entrepreneurs. SEWA is mainly financed through membership fees. Other sources of funding come from fee-based services that SEWA offers and services provided by government and non-government projects. This case study is based on information provided directly by SEWA.

The approach

SEWA uses an integrated and demand-based approach that combines addressing households' social and economic issues with developing interventions led by women based on local needs and opportunities in order to build resilience and support the "village economy". It relates to the "100 mile" concept, which suggests that if the six basic needs of daily life – food, clothing, housing, health, education and banking – can be met locally within a 100-mile area, people will find diverse and innovative solutions to problems of poverty, exploitation and environment degradation.

With regard to agriculture and food production, SEWA applied the same principle, creating small industries and providing a range of decent employment and self-employment opportunities, e.g. in processing, marketing and extension services. One example is the establishment of RUDI, a rural distribution network, in rural areas. A district association procures agricultural products that are in demand in local markets, such as spices, pulses and cereals (e.g. chili, sesame, wheat, gram dal), and transports them to a district processing centre to be cleaned, processed and packaged by local women. RUDI saleswomen ("RUDIBEN") buy the products from the processing centre and sell them directly to households in villages. There are 5 000 young women and girls engaged in RUDI activities. They get opportunities to earn an income not only as saleswomen in villages, but also by giving training in ICT and other technology and modern equipment to local farmers.

A central component of engaging with youth is skills development, particularly in technical and leadership skills. SEWA established a youth development programme, which includes the creation of education centres in rural districts and villages. These education centres offer both basic and advanced courses in subjects that are in demand among girls in the local area as well as within the market. These courses take a small fee to promote sustainability of the programme. The courses have placement units, entitled Rozgar Kendras, that focus on connecting SEWA girls and youth residing in the local community with real-life internships or employment opportunities. The Rozgar Kendras organise in-house talks and interviews for internships, and aim to achieve 100% placement in meaningful employment for young people.

Results

SEWA in Rajasthan began a youth development programme in order to help girls become local leaders. The adolescent poor in Rajasthan come from extremely conservative societies that often impose barriers to girls' development and education. SEWA grassroots leaders carried out awareness campaigns across slum areas and held in-depth family and community meetings in order to convince parents and students that girls should engage in the programme, noting the skills and personal development and potential job opportunities for girls.

Currently, 2 000 girls are working as master trainers to give training to grassroots members. In addition, 150 young women were recruited by the Rajasthan headquarter office as training and administration staff for the association. The trained girls are working in all sectors in SEWA enterprises, and are also getting jobs outside the organisation. In addition, girls are prepared for employment through SEWA-organised exposure visits that bring adolescents into contact with successful professionals and businesses.

Success factors

- **Localised actions:** Setting up schools and training centres locally within a reasonable distance to support a cluster of 5-7 villages, and identifying livelihood opportunities in the nearby vicinity
- **Tackling social norms:** Creating awareness among households of the importance and added value of sending girls to educational and vocational training
- **Targeted skills training:** Building the capacity of young girls in business management and in ICT skills.

Advisory services and market linkages to farmers through ICT, Ghana

Beneficiaries' profile: Young farmers

Number of youth beneficiaries: 5 222 farmers, the majority of whom are aged 15-35; 75% are male

ICT has not only revolutionised agricultural practices but has also empowered small and marginal farmers to access information and knowledge. Youth are early adopters of new ideas and technologies, and ICTs present a unique solution to connect and attract young people to opportunities in agriculture. A publication from the Technical Centre for Agricultural and Rural Cooperation ACP-EU (CTA) shows how several young graduates – most of them from rural farming communities – are using ICTs to provide smallholder farmers with a range of services across Africa, including training and market information (CTA, 2016).

The approach

In Ghana, the company SavaNet, owned by a young graduate with previous experience in agricultural development, aims to support young farmers. It creates platforms that connect famers with both agricultural experts and fellow farmers, obtaining up-to-date information about farming. In order to improve agricultural extension services, SavaNet provides an audio conferencing platform where farmers can call in to get the latest information about their agricultural production. In addition, SavaNet has a podcast series focused on topics that directly benefit farmers, and an agricultural GPS data service for farmers who want to better understand the geography and topography of their farms. In collaboration with the Ministry of Food and Agriculture, SavaNet aggregates early morning prices from local markets and then sends them to interested farmers via SMS, so the farmers can be sure to get the best prices.

Results

In 2014, 5 222 farmers worked with SavaNet. The majority of the SavaNet farmers are aged between 15 and 35, and about 75% are male. SavaNet's engagement with young farmers has led to the creation of primary, secondary and tertiary farmer groups at the community, district and regional levels. These farmer groups are contributing immensely in actively engaging young people in farming as a business and sustainable livelihood.

Success factors

- **Modernising farming:** Using simple ICT, SavaNet was able to provide quick and accurate information to thousands of farmers. ICT-based tools are also appealing for younger generations and make farming more modern and attractive to young people.

- **Peer role models:** SavaNet targeted young farmers who then served as role models for other hesitant rural youth. The founder of SavaNet, Moses Nganwani Tia, describes the initiative well: *"I think if other young people see their peers re-engaging in farming, they'll join them. The best way for us to get young people involved in agriculture is to highlight the young people who are already in agriculture"* (CTA, 2016).

Box 2.1. Youth-owned inclusive businesses in the agricultural sector

Agro Mindset (http://www.agromindset.com)

Ghanaian entrepreneur David Asare Asiamah is the founder of Agro Mindset, a mission-driven firm specialising in agribusiness ventures. The focus of the group is to run highly profitable farm-based enterprises with long-term growth potential and to showcase this know-how to the youth and private sector in an industry-relevant manner. The company emphasises sustainable development, value chains, entrepreneurship and "farming as a business" which lends support services to entrepreneurs in the valuation and planning of value-added agriculture. David was named in 2016 by Forbes as one of Africa's 30 most promising entrepreneurs under 30.

Sooretul (https://www.sooretul.com/)

Senegalese entrepreneur and IT engineer Awa Caba is the co-founder of Sooretul.

> Sooretul, which means "it's not far" in Awa's native language, Wolof, is an online sales platform that sells locally produced and processed food. The platform connects small-scale producers and agro-processing enterprises with the increasingly demanding middle-class Senegalese. The website started with 150 agri-food products and within a few years of launching was offering over 300 selections. Sooretul won the 2015 Rebranding Africa Award and the 2016 Pitch AgriHack.
>
> **Stawi Foods and Fruits** (http://stawiindustries.com/)
>
> Kenyan entrepreneur Eric Muthomi founded Stawi Foods and Fruits, an innovative start-up which procures bananas from smallholder farmers in rural Kenya and processes them into banana flour. The company diversified its products and now engages in several value chains, including maize, millet, sorghum, sweet potato, amaranth, wheat and soybeans. Stawi's agro-processing business creates employment for youth and enables smallholder farmers to market their produce.

Integrating rural youth into agri-food processing activities will require skills training and youth ownership

Community-driven agribusiness enterprise development, Nigeria

Beneficiaries' profile: Poorest of the poor in the rural areas of the Niger Delta, in particular, youth aged 18-35

Number of youth beneficiaries: 35 365

The Community-Based Natural Resource Management Programme (CBNRMP) is an IFAD-supported project which aims to improve the livelihoods and living conditions of rural families in the nine states of the Niger Delta region of Nigeria. While the overall target group was the poorest in rural areas, the project developed a specific targeting strategy to support youth (aged 18-35) and women in agribusiness. The value chains were selected based on the abundance and diversity of natural resources in the project area. They included crop production, artisanal fisheries, and aquaculture/cage fisheries.

The approach

The project adapted the initial community-driven development (CDD) approach to suit the objective of agribusiness development and design a pathway for youth to create their enterprises. This modification generated a huge youth response. The CDD agribusiness model combines different levels of institutions: youth individual enterprises, commodity groups and Commodity Apex Development Associations (CADAs). In parallel, the project facilitated the creation of incubation centres and a youth forum, which they named the Youth Agriculture Foundation.

The starting point of this pathway for youth was the elaboration of agro-enterprise protocols, which include the following:

- mapping/targeting high-value, low-risk, market-led, high-return enterprises; identifying youth-based commodity groups and selecting interested youth based on endorsement of the community leadership and agreement to belong to a commodity group of his/her interest

- providing two weeks' hands-on training to acquire the requisite skills for enterprise management; identifying agribusiness of candidate's choice based on self-analysis, preparation of bankable business plan and candidate's choice of ownership type

- establishing a formal agreement (e.g. a memorandum of understanding) between the youth and commodity groups on terms of engagement, including responsibility to commodity groups, repayment of revolving microcredit (matching grant) to the group, etc.

- providing starter packs (interest-free revolving loans) through the commodity groups or apex groups (which also provide a mini platform for knowledge sharing and allow common access to inputs at a moderate cost).

- linking with service providers and implementation support (monitoring, supervision, technical backstopping).

Successful enterprises become incubation hubs, clustering unemployed youth as apprentices around them and providing the youth with hands-on practical training in enterprise identification, planning, budgeting, establishment and management. At the time of the project's completion (2015), it had created over 100 successful champions/mentors in the programme area. Each of them has weaned an average of five young people who are successfully operating their enterprises and clustering/mentoring other young agripreneurs. All the parent enterprises also serve as training and excursion sites for primary and secondary school students and other new entrepreneurs.

In each community, a CADA is created as an umbrella organisation of different commodity groups. A minimum of two and a maximum of three representatives from each group within a benefiting community come together to form the community-level CADA. The functions of the CADA include the co-ordination and supervision of agripreneurs and commodity groups, facilitation of access to agro-inputs and loans, and facilitation of market access. They also provide a social guarantee to young entrepreneurs who intend to access financial credit through commodity groups or village savings and credit groups.

Results

A total of 63 858 jobs were created in on-farm and off-farm activities, employing 20 462 young men and 14 903 young women. Off-farm activities included agro-processing, marketing activities and fabricating agricultural equipment. The project classified the enterprises as strong (those with annual net profit of >NGN 500 000), moderate (NGN 100 000 to NGN 500 000) or weak (<NGN 100 000). The strong enterprises constitute 21.6% out of the total 1 000 enterprises in the sample, moderate enterprises constitute 67%, and weak enterprises constitute 13%. The best-performing enterprises were those in rice, yam and cassava processing and fisheries and poultry.

Table 2.4. Enterprise performance, by revenue

Strong	Medium	Weak
Rice, cassava, fish, yams, palm oil, poultry	All value chains with a high portion of cassava and rice	Piggery, vegetable and honey production

Source: IFAD (2016a), Community-Based Natural Resources Management Programme in the Niger Delta Region: Project Completion Report.

Figure 2.1. Number of agro-enterprises promoted, by value chain

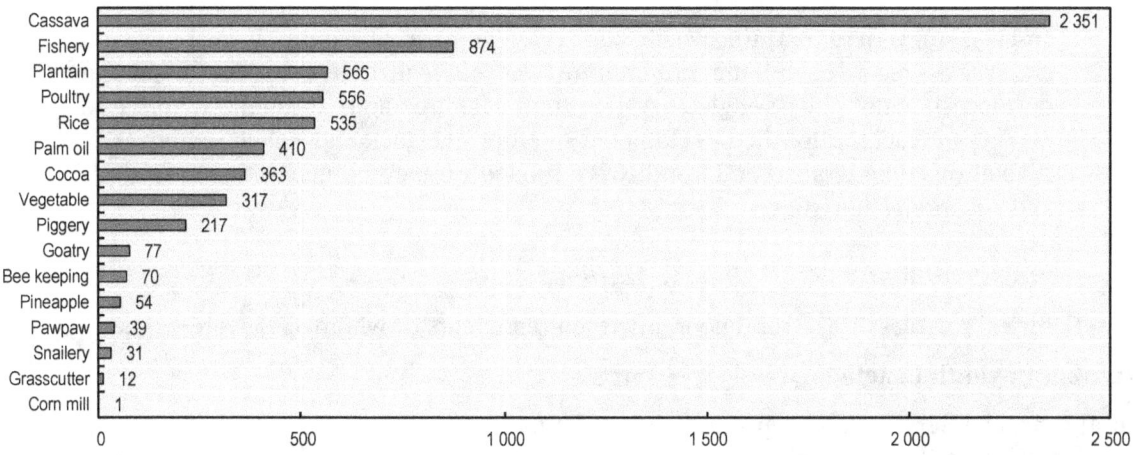

Source: IFAD (2016a), Community-Based Natural Resources Management Programme in the Niger Delta Region: Project Completion Report.

The project emphasised production-level enterprises until the last two years of the project, when it shifted activities to processing. The pipeline and follow up project, the Rural Agribusiness Sector Enhancement Programme, will build on the lessons of CBNRMP and focus on value addition through processing.

Success factors

- **The CDD approach to business development:** Building on the social capital already formed at the community level, the programme created awareness of different segments of the community, helping them to view agriculture as a business, strengthened farmer groups, and institutionalised the CADA as an umbrella association to support the enterprise groups in each community.

- **Attitude and behaviour change:** The programme's combination of intensive sensitisation, capacity building, training, mentorship and counselling built understanding and trust, transformed the mindset of the farmers from subsistence farming to agribusiness, and enabled youth to see agro-enterprises as a profitable source of livelihood.

- **Fast returns on investment:** Youth are ready to engage in agriculture if the activities will generate a high return on investment, have a short gestation period, confer business ownership to them and lead to social linkage opportunities. The gestation period is 3 months for bee keeping and rice production, 5 months for fish at 1 kg market weight, and 3.5 months for broiler at 1.2 kg market weight.

- **Mentorship and role models:** Champions and mentors in the programme were key to attracting unemployed youth and motivating them to engage in agro-businesses. Successful enterprises became incubation hubs, taking on youth as apprentices and providing them with hands-on practical training in enterprise identification, planning, budgeting, establishment and management.

- **Economies of scale:** A minimum economic scale for those enterprises was also established for smallholder farmers to come out of poverty within two years, as well as to create an inducement for youth to engage in agriculture. For example, the minimum economic size was 250 birds for poultry, 2 ha for cassava, 1 000 fingerlings for fishery and 0.25 ha for vegetables (double cropping each year).

- **In-class and field training:** The huge involvement of youth in agri-business enterprises recorded by the programme was also attributed to the linkage it developed with the Songhai Agricultural Centre and through field-based classroom teaching for the development of crop, livestock and fishery enterprises. A total of 2 984 women and youth were trained on income generation, life skills and vocational activities.

Integrating commodity value chains, Moldova

Beneficiaries' profiles: 1 815 rural poor, micro-entrepreneurs of whom 37% were women

Number of youth beneficiaries: 445

Rural Financial Services and Agricultural Development is an IFAD project which aims to sustainably contribute to the alleviation of poverty through increased income and improved livelihoods. Activities include the creation of production assets through access to investment loans and market-derived rural infrastructure; sustainable integration into commodity value chains through access to advanced production technologies and reliable post-harvest services; and the generation of employment opportunities for the rural poor.

The approach

The project simultaneously developed the upstream (increased production) and downstream (post-harvest and market access services) segments of the value chain, and adopted a demand-based approach for loans. Given the long gestation periods of fruit tree plantations, there was a higher share of investment in the upstream segment of the value chain (81%) compared with the downstream segment (19%). Contract farming was promoted to build synergies with active partners in the downstream segment of the value chain who are in need of reliable supplies (in quantity and quality) of primary commodities.

Results

The project resulted in significant agriculture productivity and income increases compared with traditional production systems. The per capita production of fruits and berries increased by 29% from 106 kg in 2011 to 137 kg in 2015. The estimated average increases in net income for nine financial models across category of beneficiary and economic activity were 7-9-fold for bee keeping, 2.5-6-fold for table grape production, 4-fold for conservation agriculture, 3-fold for a 20 ha medium-size farmer investing in a set of farm machinery, 1.8-fold for a 5 ha small farmer investing in a small tractor, and 1.8-fold for a livestock producer investing in three dairy cows. In terms of employment, permanent and seasonal job creation was considerable. The cumulative full-time equivalent jobs generated by the project directly and indirectly amounted to 5 324 households, or three times the number of direct beneficiaries.

Success factors

- **Investing upstream in the value chain:** The significant incremental production contributed to increased yields and expansion of the area for fruit trees and vegetable production, and enhanced the availability of food per capita for urban consumers. The exported products contributed to improving the import/export food trade balance.

- **Linking value chain actors:** The promotion of contract farming allowed 15 producer groups to link up to partners in post-harvest value chains.

- **Strengthening institutions:** The project built the capacities of participating financial institutions, savings and credit associations, contract farming producer groups, and users' associations in charge of the operation and maintenance of shared facilities and services developed by the project.

Increasing youth engagement in agriculture, Northern Uganda

Beneficiaries' profiles: Vulnerable youth living in the Lango, Acholi and West Nile sub-regions

Number of youth beneficiaries:

The UK's Department for International Development (DFID)-funded Transforming the Economy through Climate Smart Agri-Business Market Development (NU-TEC MD) programme aims to integrate rural youth into agricultural value chains. NU-TEC MD's role is to broker the relationship between the private sector and youth producer groups and co-operatives. Besides strengthening the private sector supply chain, the programme intended to build a sustainable relationship between the private sector and service providers, thereby enhancing continuous business engagement (Okelai et al., 2017).

The approach

A study was done to understand youth engagement in agriculture and find better ways to link youth to the private sector. The study selected sunflower and soybean markets and the interconnected markets of seed, land preparation, storage and aggregation as entry points for youth in the agricultural economy of Northern Uganda. The study identified business models in areas where youth have incentives to actively participate and where there is a business case for firms to pursue practices that are more inclusive for youth.

Results

The study proposes the following youth engagement strategies:

1. **Youth-led mechanisation for land opening and on-farm operations.** This can build around a service-led intervention model to enable youth to invest in mechanisation services as a business.

2. **Youth engagement in local seed businesses and distribution agencies.** Youth can be engaged in specialised agricultural production ventures, such as seed production, and as commissioned agents for input delivery and distribution systems.

3. **Youth engagement in production through demand-driven approaches to harness youth energy.** Youth can be supported to engage in contract farming built on commitment-based forward contract arrangements with oilseed buyers/processors.

4. **Youth participation in storage and aggregation markets.** Youth can function as buying agents or delivery agents in cases of input trading systems. For instance, the company engages youth as buying agents and facilitates them through pre-financing and mentoring. To improve the link between production and aggregation, youth producer groups can be supported with the provision of small bulking houses, and youth groups can act as primary aggregation centres.

Success factors

- **Group approach:** Interventions to facilitate private sector engagement with youth should not target youth in isolation, but as part of a group. This is a condition to ensure the sustainability of the facilitation strategy when youth transition into adulthood.

- **Working with existing and established co-operatives and associations:** Youth who could benefit from robust inclusion are those who are fully integrated into current farming structures in the community, which are producer groups, co-operatives and savings associations. Operating within the context of the existing institutional and social structures provides youth with credibility and is more likely to attract the private sector.

- **Role models:** A strong point in the current business models is that they hinge upon using role models to offer peer learning support and apprenticeship learning for youth to engage in farming as a business and adopt good agricultural practices.

- **Training and mentoring:** In addition to providing specific life and technical skills to youth producers' groups, dedicated training and mentoring are provided to youth co-operative staff to strengthen the institutional capabilities of co-operatives and allow their transition to business entities and one-stop shops for the youth producer groups.

Conclusion

A defining characteristic of most developing countries is the relative importance of agriculture in their national economies. In light of the continued growth in demand for value-added food and agriculture products, the increased attention on developing agro-industries as a sector of growth and employment creation is well justified. Looking forward, the challenge is to enable small-scale farmers and low-skilled rural youth to integrate into local and global agricultural value chains and move up the ladder to meet the quantity and quality standards required for national and export markets.

Examples described in this chapter show different interventions at the local level that can help integrate rural youth into the agricultural value chain and provide them with decent employment opportunities. The majority of examples are in the production phase, as it has the lowest barrier to entry in the value chain. Indeed, the mechanisation of agriculture promotes the creation of attractive jobs for youth in rural areas, such as tractor drivers or mechanics for agricultural machinery. Some successful examples of jobs in service provision using ICT and agro-processing are starting to emerge. Strategies that support small- and medium-size processing enterprises can generate productive employment for youth and provide a market for smallholder famers. This can create employment in low- and medium-skilled jobs while also attracting educated young entrepreneurs to invest in and/or manage these enterprises.

Applying a youth employment lens to agricultural value chain development means to purposefully set youth inclusion and youth employment as an objective. The success factors for integrating youth into agricultural value chains based on the above examples have been summarised as follows:

Rural youth profiling: Understanding the nature and conditions under which the different youth groups are engaged or excluded, and the generational and power dynamics along the value chains, will help identify the bottlenecks to be addressed when designing a youth-sensitive agricultural value chain project. This means profiling the rural youth population by age group (e.g. 15-17 year-olds will have different challenges, aspirations and skill sets than 18-35 year-olds), gender, education and skills level, social capital, access to land and finance, prevailing social norms, etc.

Selection of high-potential value chain: Young people should be involved in identifying a list of potential activities in their village and region which they see themselves capable of doing, and which at the same time represent potential growth sectors.

Mentorship and role models: Young people need role models to look up to and follow. Agriculture is associated with hardship and poverty and is considered an unattractive option for young people. Local leaders and other youth farmers can help change the mentality of rural youth through mentoring and coaching. Mentoring can happen through incubator approaches, where young farmers learn how to operate a business, or through regular meetings and interactions.

Peer-to-peer learning: The most effective way to convince young people is through other young people. Peer to peer learning has proven effective when providing agricultural extension services, for example. Recently, an increasing number of young people with higher education are starting agri-food businesses. They serve as models for other young people and play an important role in creating and investing in small industries in rural areas, building networks, and generating employment.

Awareness campaigns: The potential of agriculture and value addition is largely underestimated. Young people in rural areas need to be informed about the different activities possible along the value chain if their minds are to be changed about agriculture and related jobs. Campaigns should include information about market requirements, product standards, knowledge, innovative tools and new production methods.

Skills training: The majority of rural youth are early school dropouts and have low skills. Programmes that provide apprenticeship and on-the-job training opportunities for rural youth can increase their employability. Vocational training programmes must also consider teaching soft skills in addition to basic literacy and numeracy skills. Improving entrepreneurship skills, for example, entails training not only in business management but also in negotiation, leadership and team building.

Physical proximity: Activities must take place close to young people's homes. This is especially relevant for young women who cannot travel far to attend training or take up a job.

Financial or in-kind capital: Access to land for young people is difficult and rural areas are underserved by formal financial institutions. Furthermore, financial services are not adapted to the specific needs and constraints of youth (e.g. lack of collateral and financial resources). For youth below the age of 18, it is even more difficult and often impossible to access financial support. Activities aimed at helping young people engage in agriculture will need to support their access to land, seed capital and/or materials to get started. Access to land, in particular, will be a critical decision factor for the youth, whether to engage in farm or non-farm activities and/or to migrate.

Social capital: Agriculture is foremost about know-how and linkages with actors along the value chain; young people tend to lack both. Joining farmers' organisations or co-operatives will help youth gain trust and solidarity, as well as make access to quality inputs, services, financing and markets easier. Agricultural co-operatives have proven to be an effective mechanism for engaging young people in agriculture and increasing social capital and employment opportunities through on-farm and off-farm activities

(MIJARC/IFAD/FAO, 2012). However, hierarchical structures, high membership fees, access to land, and other co-operative membership conditions which young people cannot meet exclude them from benefiting from these organised structures.

Modern agriculture and rural areas: For agriculture to become attractive to young people it has to be less labour-intensive and use modern technology. This can not only be in the form of mechanisation, such as tractors or improved post-harvest management techniques, but also through the use of ICT to have better access to information, services and markets. Basic infrastructure (electricity, water, road, Internet) will need to be improved for young people if rural livelihoods are to become more attractive to them. Some ICTs allow young entrepreneurs to start new businesses in service provision along the agricultural value chains.

Identifying employment opportunities along agricultural value chains requires taking into account the potential the location offers in terms of natural resources and markets, as well as the profiles of young men and women. If the local context is not conducive to agriculture (i.e. lack of availability of land and water, difficult access to markets), the better option for youth will be to find a job outside the agricultural sector, e.g. in construction, ecotourism or small-scale manufacturing. In this case, the focus will need to be on building youth's employability skills needed by local enterprises and ensuring decent pay and working conditions. In addition, employers need to feel confident about recruiting youth (for example, through supervised internships, partnerships with placement organisations, and incentives from the government).

Investing in the development of secondary towns would also offer new markets to promising local value chains while creating job opportunities in the service and retail sector. Furthermore, it is crucial to understand consumer demands, global and local market competition and prices and trade policies when thinking of creating businesses from the ground up.

Countries must think strategically about how to position themselves with respect to market competition while ensuring that business models are inclusive of small-scale producers and local businesses operated by rural youth. In particular, promoting jobs downstream in the agricultural value chain requires higher-skilled young people on the supply side, while at the same time boosting the demand side through a mix of market-based policies and identification of specific sectors or industries with comparative advantages. The next chapter is dedicated to policy interventions to support rural youth employment demand along the agricultural value chain.

Notes

[1] The farmer's organisation sponsors a young man or woman who will receive inputs through a sliding financing system; otherwise, all members of the organisation receive training on good agricultural practices.

References

Allen, T. and P. Heinrigs (2016), "Emerging opportunities in the West African food economy", *West African Papers*, No. 1, OECD Publishing, Paris, http://dx.doi.org/10.1787/5jlvfj4968jb-en.

Allen, T., P. Heinrigs and I. Heo (2018), "Agriculture, food and jobs in West Africa", *West African Papers*, No. 14, OECD Publishing, Paris, http://dx.doi.org/10.1787/dc152bc0-en.

Balse, M. et al. (2015), "Une expérience originale de mécanisation partagée en Afrique. Les Coopératives d'utilisation de matériel agricole au Bénin" (An innovative organizational approach for West African family farmer co-operative: the case of mechanization cooperatives (CUMAs) in Benin), Food and Agriculture Organization, Rome.

CTA (2016), *Innovate for Agriculture: Young ICT Entrepreneurs Overcoming Challenges and Transforming Agriculture*, Technical Centre for Agricultural and Rural Cooperation, Wageningen, Netherlands.

FAO (2014), "FAO, private and public partnership model for youth employment in agriculture: Experiences from Malawi, Tanzania Mainland and Zanzibar archipelago", *Case Study Series*, No. 4, Food and Agriculture Organization of the United Nations, Rome.

Hathie, I. (28 April 2014), "Youth unemployment: A potential destabilizing force in Senegal?", Africa Up Close: a blog of the Africa Program at the Wilson Center, https://africaupclose.wilsoncenter.org/youth-unemployment-a-potential-destabilizing-force-in-senegal/.

IFAD (2016a), *Community-Based Natural Resources Management Programme (CBNRMP) in the Niger Delta Region: Project Completion Report*, IFAD West and Central Africa Division.

IFAD (2016b), Projet d'Appui aux Filieres Agricoles (PAFA). Rapport de supervision. Département gestion des programmes.

MIJARC/IFAD/FAO (2012), "Summary of the findings of the project implemented by MIJARC in collaboration with FAO and IFAD: 'Facilitating access of rural youth to agricultural activities'", The Farmers' Forum Youth Session, 18 February 2012, Rome.

OECD (2017), *Unlocking the Potential of Youth Entrepreneurship in Developing Countries: From Subsistence to Performance*, Development Centre Studies, OECD Publishing, Paris, http://dx.doi.org/10.1787/9789264277830-en.

OECD Development Centre (2018), *Youth Well-being Policy Review of Malawi*, EU-OECD Youth Inclusion Project, Paris, https://www.oecd.org/countries/malawi/Youth-well-being-policy-review-Malawi.pdf.

OECD Development Centre (2017a), *Youth Well-being Policy Review of Cambodia*, EU-OECD Youth Inclusion Project, Paris, https://www.oecd.org/countries/cambodia/Youth-well-being-policy-review-Cambodia.pdf.

OECD Development Centre (2017b), *Youth Well-being Policy Review of Côte d'Ivoire*, EU-OECD Youth Inclusion Project, Paris, http://www.oecd.org/dev/inclusivesocietiesanddevelopment/Examen-du%20bien-etre-et-des-politiques-de-la-jeunesse-en-Cote-dIvoire.pdf.

OECD Development Centre (2017c), *Youth Well-being Policy Review of Viet Nam*, EU-OECD Youth Inclusion Project, Paris, http://www.oecd.org/dev/inclusivesocietiesanddevelopment/OECDYouthReportVietNam_ebook.pdf.

Okelai, J.A. et al. (2017), "Increasing youth engagement in agriculture in Northern Uganda: Situation report and proposed strategies", *NU-TEC Market Development Programme: A study to support better understanding of youth in agriculture in Northern Uganda*, Royal Tropical Institute, Amsterdam.

Shimeles, A. (2010), "Migration patterns, trends and policy issues in Africa", *Working Paper Series*, No. 119, African Development Bank Group, Tunis, Tunisia.

UN (2016), *UN report of the FAO/ILO sponsored Rapid Market Assessment conducted in view of proposing optimal value chains for UN's engagement in job creation*, Sub-sector Selection report of August 2016, United Nations, New York.

UNESCAP (2016), *Economic and Social Survey of Asia and the Pacific 2015: Year-End Update*, United Nations Economic and Social Commission for Asia and the Pacific, Bangkok.

USAID (2015), *Mali Out-of-School Youth Project's Final Report*, U.S. Agency for International Development, Washington, DC.

World Bank (2007), *The World Development Report 2008: Agriculture for Development*, The International Bank for Reconstruction and Development/The World Bank, Washington, DC.

Chapter 3. Towards decent work opportunities for rural youth

Without structural transformation happening fast enough in rural areas to create more employment in a sustainable manner, the vast majority of rural youth in developing countries have little choice but to be self-employed in the informal sector, take up poorly paid jobs, or migrate for better opportunities. The increasing demand for diversified and processed food in developing countries is, however, offering the opportunity for rural economies to create various types of jobs along the agricultural value chains, both upstream and downstream. This chapter provides recommendations to policy makers in adopting a comprehensive and local approach to rural economic development to make rural areas attractive again to young people.

Providing decent jobs for youth has become a national priority in both Organisation for Economic Co-operation and Development (OECD) and non OECD countries. The youth bulge is a common phenomenon in many developing countries, and needs to be addressed urgently. In Africa, particularly in sub-Saharan Africa, the youth population will continue to increase until 2050. Without structural transformation and green industrialisation happening fast enough to create more wage employment in a sustainable manner, the vast majority of youth in developing countries have little choice but to be self-employed in the informal sector or take up poorly paid jobs, without any social protection and hope for better job prospects. The challenge is particularly acute for rural youth, who still represent the majority of youth in developing countries. Yet, rural economies are transforming slowly. In order to absorb this growing young rural labour force, opportunities in rural areas and intermediary and small towns must become attractive and include decent wages and incomes and prospects for better lives.

In recent years, household dietary pattern changes, coupled with new demands by a rising middle class for diversified and processed foods, are creating off-farm employment in food-related manufacturing and services. Agri-food industries are labour-intensive and can create jobs in rural areas, as well as ensure food security in the regions. Food processing is particularly relevant for job creation in rural areas because agro-industries (e.g. millers, beer breweries, processors) are more likely than other sectors to locate in small towns and rural areas and not in primary cities (Christiaensen and Lawin, 2017; Henderson and McNamara, 2000;). In addition, food processing creates strong forward and backward linkages with other food and non-food system activities, implying potentially large wage employment effects in local economies. Furthermore, the agri-food processing sector tends to employ low-skilled labour, providing wage job opportunities for the current large number of low-educated rural youth and rural women in developing countries.

In this context, the employment landscape along the agricultural value chains represents a huge untapped opportunity of entrepreneurship, business development and wage labour. However, value chain development projects seldom apply an employment lens, and even less a youth employment lens. Their objectives are usually about increasing revenues and export volumes, meeting consumer needs and improving efficiencies along the supply chains. Value chain analyses consider only partially the consequences on poverty, inequality, food security and environment (Bolwig et al., 2010). In fact, young entrepreneurs in sub-Saharan Africa are reluctant to become involved in agriculture as a business (Kew, 2015).

Governments can play an important role in enacting legislation and implementing regulations; providing incentives, support schemes and standards to identify and promote agricultural value chains that create farm and non-farm employment for youth. The creation of new job opportunities downstream in the value chain, in food processing and distribution for example, can help keep young people in the sector. For this to happen, governments need to design policies that take into account the constraints and priorities of rural young men and women. This chapter provides some policy recommendations on how to support agricultural and local value chain development as well as non-farm activities, with the objective of creating rural youth employment.

Promoting local value chains as an engine for the creation of decent youth jobs and food security

Although the focus of value chain development has often been on higher-value products for trade in more lucrative and export markets, processes of value chain development are also significant in domestic and basic food production chains. Global value chains tend to exclude a large proportion of farmers, especially smallholders, as they face a range of constraints, e.g. small size of production unit; lack of information, knowledge, financial means, and capacity to comply with the requirements, food regulation, and quality standard of global markets; and price volatility. With the appropriate support (technology, finance, training), the development of local value chains holds opportunities for small farmers as producers to be linked with small- and medium-sized businesses and markets, and for the creation of wage labour – for example in service provision and agro-processing (see Chapter 2).

The growing domestic demand in agri-food products, both for quantity and diversity, is largely underexploited. Different value chains entail different opportunities and the cost of entering some value chains, such as those in the export market, is probably too high for the majority of small-scale farmers. The challenge is greater for young people living in rural areas in developing countries because they are largely unskilled and low educated, with limited access to land, credit and information on market opportunities. Promoting local value chain development is not only necessary for youth inclusion but also for ensuring food security in the context of rapid urbanisation, increasing dependence on food and feed imports, and growing domestic demands. Youth involvement in a local value chain can happen in several ways.

Promoting an entire value chain requires actions at the macro, meso and micro levels and better co-ordination between actors along the value chain. At the macro level, there are regulatory frameworks, national development strategies and trade policies that will support or hinder certain value chains (see Box 3.1). At the meso level, there are industry standards and businesses that will determine the channels and efficiencies of the value chains. At the micro level, there are small-scale producers and young people who need capacity building, skills and equipment upgrades, and access to capital in order to integrate into the value chain as self-employed workers or wage workers (see Chapter 2). Using a value chain approach to development means working on all three levels at the same time. For example, creating incentives for the private sector to provide the necessary goods and services to small-scale producers can help the latter integrate into the value chain as suppliers or business partners. At the same time, improving the efficiency and capacity of processors or other downstream actors can create additional demand and higher prices for crops, with direct benefits for small-scale producers (IFAD, 2014a).

> **Box 3.1. Selecting the right value chain: A chicken-and-egg problem**
>
> With the growing urban demand for diversified food, especially in meat, cities in the African continent represent a huge market potential for locally produced agricultural products. African chicken consumption for example has risen sharply over the past two decades. Imports of chicken to sub-Saharan Africa tripled between 2004 and 2014, according to data from the US Department of Agriculture. However, the rising demand has been met by increased imports from the European Union, Brazil and the United States and not by increased local supply and job creation. In fact, local poultry farmers have not been able to compete against the flood of cheap frozen imports and are closing down. In particular, bone-in frozen chicken portions – an unpopular part of the chicken in developed countries – are dumped into the market at very low prices.
>
> Poultry farming requires large quantities of maize and soya, which often have to be imported at a high cost. Ghanaian poultry farmer Napoleon Oduro runs a 500-bird farm on the outskirts of Accra. He relies on imported feed, which costs him a as much as USD 625 per month to feed his 500 birds (each bird requires about 2.5 kg of feed per month and 50 kg of feed costs USD 50). African chickens are also a different breed from imported ones and they require more feed and are less productive.
>
> Despite the stiff competition, African poultry farmers are not giving up. Many are getting informed about better breeds and are looking for local ingredients to substitute traditional chicken feed. Other business opportunities exist in processing by products (pre-cooked meat) and investing in broiler breeding facilities. To protect local industries, some countries such as Botswana have imposed import restrictions, but in the long run the problem will need to be resolved by strengthening the overall agricultural systems in Africa.
>
> First and foremost, investing in low-cost and high-quality feed production will be needed. Stronger phytosanitary regulations and disease control must be enforced to protect the animals from infectious diseases. Infrastructure (energy, roads and transport, cold storage facilities, water distribution) must be significantly improved, especially in rural areas, in order for the poultry industry to be productive and meet the rising demand from cities in terms of quality and quantity. There is also limited research in agriculture in the continent. Research to support breeding programmes and expand the range of feed sources will go a long way in helping to upgrade the overall system. African governments need to make a leap in modernising the agricultural system, including through research, while ensuring sustainable practices.
>
> Solving the chicken-and-egg problem will require striking the right balance between imports, responsible local consumption and production while preventing unfair trade practices and ensuring sustainable poultry farming.

Currently, in developing countries, many value chain interventions are at the primary production level, as seen in Chapter 2. Production has a lower entry barrier than downstream activities and is therefore an easier sector for the more vulnerable groups to enter. However, the agro-processing industry is labour intensive and can provide opportunities to generate wage employment for young people. Highly labour-intensive value chains such as horticulture offer wage employment opportunities for landless rural youth (IFAD, 2014a). Interventions can therefore be at different points downstream in the value chain: collection, processing, transportation, wholesaling and retailing. Some jobs downstream in the value chain require higher levels of education, attracting more educated youth in managerial positions. The processes of agro-industrialisation bring about the emergence of providers of managerial and other business services (da Silva et al., 2009). Selecting the right value chain to integrate into will require fully assessing demand from consumers and understanding the power dynamics between value chain actors and pull-push factors. Whether a value chain is producer-driven or buyer-driven, for example, can impact a firm's ability to move up the ladder (AfDB/OECD/UNDP, 2014).

A crucial component of the agricultural value chain model is the presence of sufficient demand for the product being supplied, especially in urban areas which have more spending capacity. The rise of supermarkets in some developing countries changed the food market structure. The penetration of supermarkets was greatest in South Africa, South America and East Asia. The rise of supermarkets has attracted foreign direct investment (FDI) as well as set new standards for food safety and quality. Supermarkets in developing countries have also been changing their procurement strategy to shift away from wholesale procurement to specialised procurement agents, centralisation and regionalisation, and cultivating preferred suppliers to secure consistent supply. These strategies have helped in better organising the suppliers, improving the production processes, and ultimately helping to increase revenues (da Silva et al., 2009). Small-scale producers, if organised to ensure economies of scale and quality (e.g. through co-operatives), could tap into this market. However, as supermarkets take increasingly larger shares of the retail market for food, there is a definite shift of power towards a buyer-driven supply chain for processed food products. Therefore, market development must be balanced and paced so that agricultural production can increase without crowding out small-scale producers. The 2008 *World Development Report* calls for inclusive procurement systems in integrated supply chains and supermarkets, so that small-scale farmers can share in these growth opportunities (World Bank, 2007).

The focus on strengthening local value chains based on sustainable use of mainly local resources can also contribute to reducing the dietary dependence on imported food and prioritising local foods for domestic markets, including growing tourist markets in certain countries. Local food markets are also one of the key mechanisms to enhance access to and availability of food. The International Planning Committee for Food Sovereignty specifies four pillars of food sovereignty: the right to food; access to productive resources such as land, water, forest, fisheries, seeds and capital; mainstreaming agroecological production based on local and renewable resources and the preservation of natural resources; and access to trade and local markets. Finally, with the concerns around energy use in the globalised food economy and the energy supply becoming short and more expensive, it is expected that locally and regionally traded food will be more competitive than imports, constituting a complementary mechanism to local production when needed (HELVETAS Swiss Intercooperation, 2013).

Reducing food loss is another pathway to improve farmers' income and uncover employment opportunities. About 40% of staple foods in sub-Saharan Africa are lost before they can reach the market (Aulakh and Regmi, 2013), with consequences on food availability and quality, scarce natural resources, greenhouse gas production, and loss of income. Total food spoilage could feed about 300 million people per year in sub-Saharan Africa (AfDB/OECD/UNDP, 2016). Food losses can occur at different stages of the supply chain, from harvesting to storage, processing, packaging and sales. They result from wide-ranging managerial and technical limitations in harvesting techniques, storage, transportation, processing, cooling facilities, packaging and marketing systems, as well as from pests and weather patterns.

Simple methods and training can improve production planning, processing, packaging and transportation practices. Cassava in Africa is a good example of the benefits of adding value to a staple crop, e.g. increase income for producers, create employment in rural areas in village processing units, and reduce the need to import wheat. In Nigeria, after harvesting, cassava tubers are transported to the processing plants in trucks. Cassava tubers must be processed within 72 hours of harvesting, due to rapid fermentation that renders them sour and unfit for consumption. As a result, harvesting typically only occurs once a guaranteed buyer is identified. This simple precaution helps to avoid food loss and increase farmer revenues.[1]

Finally, one of the critical factors of successful local value chain development is understanding the governance and power structure of the particular value chain. What are the agreed terms of trade, quality standards and pricing structure that small-scale producers and young people should know in order to assess the opportunities and risks of their engagement? The more dialogue there is with actors at all levels, the more likely the economic gains will be fairly distributed among them. Micro, small and medium enterprises are a major source of employment and income, and therefore it is important to integrate them into rural value chains. Partnerships among smaller enterprises can help gain leverage to compete with larger firms. Co-operatives of producers in this sense can help increase the bargaining power of small-scale farmers.

Linking rural and urban development using a territorial approach

Population growth, urbanisation, and economic growth present opportunities for businesses connected to the agricultural sector. Urbanisation can contribute to higher agricultural productivity and rural development, and ultimately to economic development and structural transformation, by better connecting rural economic activities (particularly food production chains) to large urban markets (AfDB/OECD/UNDP, 2016). Urbanisation plays a central role in changing Africa's food system by: 1) increasing the consumer base for food producers; 2) benefiting the post-farm food value; and 3) transforming the rural non-farm economy. More densely populated places tend to handle post-farm segments of food value chains, i.e. activities beyond primary production, such as wholesaling, processing, logistics, distribution, retail and food stalls. In Africa, the growth of towns and intermediary cities has strengthened the reciprocal linkages between rural and urban development. Reducing the travel time to the nearest city of 100 000 inhabitants from 24 to 4 hours increases the ratio of actual to potential crop production by 16. Greater agricultural production also develops the rural non-farm sector in countries at a lower stage of the post-farm food value chain, creating a virtuous circle of agricultural and rural development (AfDB/OECD/UNDP, 2016).

Focusing resources and investments on the development of secondary towns would offer new markets to small farmers and processors while creating new job opportunities for youth, including skilled youth, e.g. in the service and retail sector (Hathie, 2016). Investments should go into strengthening rural-urban linkages and intraregional trade and prioritising transport and marketing infrastructure to improve market access and value addition, reduce post-harvest losses, and expand input markets and support services in rural areas. While metropolitan areas are the main interface with global markets, small cities and towns are the main interface with the rural economy and serve as a means by which urban food habits spread into rural areas (Staatz and Hollinger, 2016). While national accounts of most countries largely ignore the economic activities of the informal sector, in most low-income countries informal or local agro-processing remains strong (da Silva et al., 2009). Furthermore, the role of supermarkets has increased rapidly, accompanied by a rise in the local demand for high-quality food products and processed food, especially in Asia. In West Africa, modern food retailing remains underdeveloped relative to the market size, urbanisation levels and economic dynamism (Allen and Heinrigs, 2016). In Africa, local agro-enterprises are increasingly engaging in the delivery of agricultural services to small-scale farmers (often as a response to weak public services). Investment such as joint ventures, contract farming with local buying and marketing groups, out-grower schemes, and infrastructure investments can have positive impacts on employment, including for youth (Arias et al., 2013), especially if they include decent work aspects (UNIDROIT/FAO/IFAD, 2015).

In Viet Nam, a study (Duteurtre et al., 2016) of value chain development in three districts (Ba Vi, Moc Chau and Mai Son) shows the different factors in the functioning of markets beyond costing and pricing to include collective organisation, access to resources and spatial organisation. Each district has a unique comparative advantage in the production of milk (Ba Vi), vegetables (Moc Chau) and maize (Mai Son), and produces for household consumption and local markets first, then for the urban markets of Hanoi.

The study concluded that the commercialisation of these products was a process that was highly dependent on the intricate linkages between producers, businesses and traders. Actors upstream and downstream in the value chains played an important role, but equally important was the role of the state. Geographic indications such as "Ba Vi milk" and "Moc Chau tea" added value to these products and helped their commercialisation. Deals were made through formal contracts, personal networks, credit arrangements or simply through the exchange of information and know-how which created trust and enabled transactions.

Increased commercialisation of products led to introducing new animal and seed varieties and diversifying the methods of production and transformation in these regions. The success of these value chains also attracted new farmers and investors who were not native to the regions. However, these changes came with new risks; increased production also meant intensification in terms of land use and capital investment, causing soil pollution and erosion as well as increased debts for farmers. The government will need to enforce strict rules and regulations for all actors along the value chain and apply limits to manage production and natural resources in a sustainable manner.

The G20 calls for the following action areas to promote secondary towns: 1) create an environment attractive for firms to locate in secondary towns, including policy incentive considerations and provision of necessary infrastructure (access roads, energy and communication); 2) create conditions that also make secondary towns attractive to young men and women to live and work there, including education, health and recreation; 3) consider territorial approaches to development in order to strengthen rural-urban linkages and maximise the use of secondary towns as key conduits to connect rural and urban business activities, focusing on jobs-intensive activities in agricultural value chains and in other processing, trade and services sectors; and 4) identify patterns of labour movements and remittance flows between rural areas, intermediary towns and urban centres to best influence the set of opportunities for young people who are integrated into a multi-local household livelihood system (World Bank/IFAD, 2017).

Adopting a comprehensive approach to rural development

Growth in productive sector wage employment will need to be stimulated in order to address youth employment challenges. The regions that have successfully increased demand for labour are those where the proportion of productive sector wage earners in total employment has been rising. Unless demand for labour expands, it is difficult to design and implement programmes to increase the inclusion of disadvantaged youth (Bennell, 2007). Investments to promote growth sectors in rural areas in line with the comparative advantage of the territory and to support access to markets can contribute to the creation of on-farm and off-farm wage employment.

FAO assists policy makers, planners and development practitioners in building more integrated interventions through an Integrated Country Approach (ICA) for decent rural employment. The ICA looks at:

- core functions such as capacity development, policy support, partnerships and knowledge generation

- policy areas such as employment, migration, sustainable agriculture and agribusiness development, gender, and social protection

- the four pillars of the International Labour Organization's (ILO's) Decent Work Agenda: employment creation and enterprise development, social protection, standards and rights at work, and governance and social dialogue

- gender equality and environmental sustainability as cross-cutting issues.

The ICA aims, in particular, to enhance the employment content of national strategies, policies and programmes for agricultural and rural development in order to optimise the contribution of the sector to improving the quantity as well as the quality of rural jobs.

The first phase of the programme was implemented in Malawi and Tanzania (2011-14), where FAO facilitated the commitment of national stakeholders to a long-term theory of change on employment, providing systematic support on decent work inclusion into the design of policies, strategies and programmes, such as the Tanzanian National Agriculture Policy (2013). In particular, technical support and capacity development were provided on youth employment and child labour prevention in agriculture.

The second phase of the ICA (2015-17) was implemented in Guatemala, Senegal and Uganda, focusing on youth as the main target group. The approach provides capacity and technical support to enhance the employment content and youth focus in policies and programmes for rural development based on country-specific contexts. For example, in Senegal, the ICA programme supports the development of a national policy on rural youth employment and its related strategy. In Uganda, with the support of the ICA programme, the government is developing a national strategy for youth in agriculture and is focusing on understanding how to integrate rural youth along agricultural value chains and ensuring that youth employment issues are integrated into other parts of strategic programmes.[2] In Guatemala, the programme targets the department of San Marcos, with the aim of increasing knowledge of youth challenges and needs and defining a rural youth employment strategy within the framework of the Implementation Plan of the National Policy of Integrated Rural Development.

The OECD calls for a New Rural Development Paradigm (NRDP) to consider the new set of challenges and opportunities that developing countries face today. The NRDP provides a framework for building rural development strategies for developing countries that are tailored to the specific socio-economic, political and institutional characteristics of each country. It adopts a multi-level and multi agent approach, recognising the different roles of national and sub national authorities and enabling adequate co-ordination mechanisms that improve the policy delivery process. This approach implies the strong involvement of sub national and local governments, as well as local communities, in designing rural development strategies.

The NRDP is based on eight components (OECD, 2016):

- **Governance.** A consistent and robust strategy is not enough if implementation capacity is weak. It is therefore important for an effective strategy to build governance capacity and integrity at all levels.
- **Multiple sectors.** Although agriculture remains a fundamental sector in developing countries and should be targeted by rural policy, rural development strategies should also promote off-farm activities and employment generation in the industrial and service sectors.
- **Infrastructure.** Improving both soft and hard infrastructure to reduce transaction costs and strengthen rural-urban linkages is a key part of any strategy in developing countries. It includes improvements in connectivity across rural areas and with secondary cities, as well as in access to education and health services.
- **Urban-rural linkages.** Rural livelihoods are dependent on the performance of urban centres for their access to goods, services and new technologies; exposure to new ideas; and temporary or even permanent employment. Successful rural development strategies do not treat rural areas as isolated entities, but rather as part of a system comprising both rural and urban areas.
- **Inclusiveness.** Government policy should explicitly target poverty and inequality in multiple dimensions (health and nutrition, education, other hard and soft infrastructure, job creation) and combat the exclusion of certain groups.
- **Gender.** Improving rural livelihoods should take into account the critical role of women in rural development, including their property rights and their ability to control and deploy resources.
- **Demography.** High fertility rates and rapidly ageing populations are two of the most relevant challenges faced by rural areas in developing countries today. Although the policy implications of these two issues are different, addressing these challenges will require good co-ordination across education, health and social protection policies, as well as family planning.
- **Sustainability.** Taking into account environmental sustainability in rural development strategies should not be limited to the high dependence of rural populations on natural resources for livelihoods and growth; it should also consider their vulnerability to climate change and threats from energy, food and water scarcity.

Rural development strategies must be at the heart of national development strategies to ensure equal, inclusive and sustainable development for all (OECD, 2016), and youth mainstreaming in these strategies will become increasingly important. It would therefore be worth adding to this list the need to disaggregate data by age groups (e.g. 15-24 or 15-29 years) when designing, implementing and measuring the results of rural development programmes.

Box 3.2. Geographical indications for territorial development

Products standards such as regional labels, organic labels or controlled designation of origin allow the recognition of a particular product coming from a specific geographic area, and could potentially support value addition and the development of local value chains in Africa and Asia. The African Union Commission, with the support of the European Union, is promoting geographical indications (GIs) as a development tool that can protect the identity of local and indigenous products throughout Africa.

GIs have attracted increasing attention from policy makers and trade negotiators, and from agricultural producers, since they were mentioned in the Agreement on Trade Related Aspects of Intellectual Property Rights (the TRIPS Agreement) in 1994. This form of intellectual property (IP) now appeals to more and more nations beyond the restricted list of countries that have traditionally pursued active GI policies. According to the World Intellectual Property Organization (WIPO), a GI is a sign used on products that have a specific geographical origin and possess qualities or a reputation that are due to that origin. In order to function as a GI, a sign must identify a product as originating in a given place. In addition, the qualities, characteristics or reputation of the product should be essentially due to the place of origin. Since the qualities depend on the geographical place of production, there is a clear link between the product and its original place of production. A GI right enables those who have the right to use the indication to prevent its use by a third party whose product does not conform to the applicable standards. For example, in the jurisdictions in which the Darjeeling GI is protected, producers of Darjeeling tea can exclude use of the term "Darjeeling" for tea not grown in their tea gardens or not produced according to the standards set out in the code of practice for the GI.

The basic concept underlying GIs is simple, and familiar to any shopper who chooses Roquefort over "blue" cheese or Darjeeling over "black" tea. "Cognac", "Scotch", "Porto", "Havana", "Tequila" and "Darjeeling" are some well-known examples of names associated throughout the world with products of a certain nature and quality, known for their geographical origin and for having characteristics linked to that origin. Kampot pepper, produced in the Kampot province in Cambodia, won GI status in 2010. Since gaining GI status, prices for Kampot pepper increased from USD 5 per kilogramme before GI status in 2010 to about USD 18 per kilogramme in 2014.

Studies show that, under appropriate conditions, GIs can contribute to development in rural areas. Regional producers become entitled to use a GI and the added value generated by the GI therefore accrues among all such producers. Because GI products usually generate a premium brand price, they contribute to local employment creation, which ultimately may help to prevent rural exodus. In addition, GI products also have important spin-off effects, for example in tourism, creating additional jobs. GIs may bring value to a region not only in terms of jobs and higher income, but also by promoting the region as a whole, contributing to the creation of a "regional brand" (WIPO, 2017). Unfortunately, research usually focuses on the impact of standards in global value chains, but rarely on those impacts in local value chains or the effects on employment.

Exploiting the opportunities in regional and international markets

Despite the large share of agriculture in gross domestic product (GDP), many developing countries are increasingly dependent on imports. About 85% of global value chain trade in value added takes place in and around three regional hubs: East Asia, Europe and North Africa (AfDB/OECD/UNDP, 2014). As an example, Africa's share of global imports in intermediate goods has remained the same at 2% since the 1990s compared with non-OECD countries which have increased from 25% to 40% on average for the same period (AfDB/OECD/UNDP, 2014). Exploiting the opportunities in regional and international markets will be essential for Africa and South/Southeast Asia to be able to tap their agricultural potential.

Global agro-industrial exports have diversified significantly since the mid-1990s towards processed and high-value horticultural products – accounting in 2008 for around half of global agro-industrial exports (three quarters if semi-processed commodities are added). In Africa, the diversity of agriculture and climate provides major opportunities for regional trade. However, currently only about 10% of agricultural trade is from within the region. Cross-border trade continues to incur high transaction costs from administrative red tape and bribes. Simplification, greater transparency and harmonisation of procedures (on export/import licences, certification of origin, standards and sanitary regulations) are required (Schaffnit Chatterjee, 2014).

A concrete example of policy facilitating the creation of export and trade channels can be found in the Sri Lankan floriculture value chain. The Ministry of Export, through an ILO-Sida project (2005-09), established a new export zone to cater for approximately 10 000 existing and potential new flower growers. Growers could import supplies duty free, improve contacts with exporters and more effectively meet their requirements thanks to an export-oriented processing and packaging plant. Nearly 100 growers boosted export earnings from close to zero to between LKR 500 and LKR 1 000 per week. Flower exports grew by an average of 9% annually over the project period, generating high net foreign exchange earnings for the country. The project is credited with impacting the value chains of an estimated 52 000 micro and small enterprises, tripling household income in the targeted districts, and increasing the employment rate by 15% in businesses in the targeted districts.

The Sri Lankan floriculture case demonstrates a more "systemic" approach to intervening in value chains. Besides creating a new export zone, the project focused on strengthening the bargaining power of flower growers through a new Tropical Floriculture Association. The association helped growers negotiate better input prices and share knowledge and marketing information. A better understanding of export markets encouraged growers to move towards meeting export standards. In addition, this organised structure helped growers access loans from banks (Barlow, 2011).

Another space for opportunities is the aquaculture sector, which is very dynamic, particularly in Asia. FAO indicates that in 2014, 84% of the global population engaged in the fisheries and aquaculture sector was in Asia, followed by Africa with barely 10% (FAO, 2016). Aquaculture provides half of all fish for human consumption. Youth are involved in aquaculture in different activities: young men are often involved as casual part-time employees (e.g. pond construction and harvesting) whereas young women, although they play a large role in post-harvest activities, are often limited to sales and marketing. Youth engagement as owner-operators of fish farms is limited, due to the entry barriers in the sector (FAO, 2014).

Worldwide, the proportion of people employed in capture fisheries decreased from 83% in 1990 to 67% in 2014, whereas the proportion of people employed in fish farming correspondingly increased from 17% to 33%. Women account for about 50% of the workforce in small-scale fisheries, particularly in processing and trade. Unfortunately, statistics largely fail to capture the youth and children working in the sector, and the limited data available are rarely disaggregated by gender. The level of intra African trade in agricultural and food products is low: By the end of the 2000s, only 17% of the total foreign trade of African countries was conducted at the intra-regional level, mainly with flows of local unprocessed products (coffee, fruits, vegetables, tobacco, etc.). Animal products (cattle and fish) are the most traded products in the different African sub regions. Cereal trade is also important. The three regional organisations – the East African Community, the Common Market for Eastern and Southern Africa and the Southern African Development Community – have been committed since 2008 to creating a vast "tripartite" free trade area.

Many developing economies in the Asia Pacific region have focused on export-led growth. In more recent years, agricultural trade between Association of Southeast Asian Nations (ASEAN) countries has increased. In 2008, ASEAN was both the major destination and origin of agricultural products in Southeast Asian countries (Chandra and Lontoh, 2010). However, there is also considerable potential for growth in domestic demand, as these economies benefit from favourable demographics in terms of younger populations, rapid urbanisation and an expanding middle class. Southeast Asian governments have opted for policies that ensure sufficient domestic production and manage the stability of food prices. Government interventions are commonly found to affect a small set of agricultural products, typically between 8 and 10 products, such as rice, cereals (e.g. wheat and maize), sugar, meat products, dairy products, vegetable oils and other agricultural products (Chandra and Lontoh, 2010).

Investing in agriculture and rural infrastructure

FAO estimates that net investments of more than USD 80 billion per year are needed if food production is to keep pace with rising demand as incomes grow and the population exceeds 9 billion in 2050. FDI flows to developing countries doubled between 2005 and 2008, but negligible amounts went to agricultural production in South Asia and sub-Saharan Africa. The bulk of FDI flows went to downstream activities in upper-middle and high-income countries (FAO, 2013). According to OECD statistics, official development assistance or agriculture and rural development declined from 24% in the 1980s (OECD, n.d.) to 8% in 2013 (OECD, 2015). The increase in agricultural commodity prices and, in particular, the food price crises of 2007 08, led to notable growth in public and private investment in primary agriculture, even if the level of national budget allocation remains low. The majority of private domestic investors are farmers and they are by far the largest source of investment in agriculture (crops, livestock, aquaculture, agroforestry) in low- and middle-income countries (Lowder, Carisma and Skoet, 2012). In 2010, only nine countries in Africa had reached or exceeded the target of allocating at least 10% of their national budget to agriculture. The average regional spending on agriculture is approximately 4% (NEPAD, 2013).

> **Box 3.3. Transforming agriculture in Africa: Is CAADP the answer?**
>
> CAADP is the African Union's strategic policy framework for the agricultural transformation of the African continent. It was established in 2003 by the African Union and the New Partnership for Africa's Development (NEPAD) in Maputo. The objective is to achieve an annual growth rate of at least 6% in agricultural GDP in every country involved through an investment of at least 10% of annual national budgets in the agricultural sector by 2015.
>
> CAADP experienced a difficult beginning. The NEPAD Secretariat acknowledges that the initiative encountered ownership issues at the country level which stalled investment in the sector by governments and development partners. It also did not have the human or financial resources or legal status to enable it to fulfil its mandate and role (NEPAD, 2013). Although CAADP's objective has not been reached, some countries (Benin, Burkina Faso, Burundi, Côte d'Ivoire, Ethiopia, Ghana, Kenya, Liberia and Malawi) have made progress and CAADP is again picking up momentum. As of today, 43 African countries have formally joined CAADP and at least 40 have developed a National Agricultural Investment Plan, presenting agriculture as a top priority.
>
> The 2014 Malabo Declaration launched the second generation of ten years of CAADP by adopting the below key commitments:
>
> - recommitment to the principles and values of the CAADP process
> - commitment to enhancing investment finance in agriculture
> - commitment to ending hunger in Africa by 2025
> - commitment to halving poverty by the year 2025 through inclusive agricultural growth and transformation
> - commitment to boosting intra African trade in agricultural commodities and services
> - commitment to enhancing the resilience of livelihoods and production systems to climate variability and other related risks
> - commitment to mutual accountability to actions and results.
>
> In the future, policy makers will need to ensure sufficient co-ordination, accountability, and compliance, as well as successful resource mobilisation, including domestic resources, to boost agricultural productivity and address food insecurity. Agricultural productivity could be increased by developing infrastructure to facilitate market access; optimise land, water, and resource management; increase agricultural research; and stimulate the private sector to unleash productive investments in the sector (Signé, 2017). Ultimately, the success of CAADP will depend on individual countries' ownership of and commitment to meeting the goals.

The United Nations Conference on Trade and Development's (UNCTAD's) survey of investment promotion agencies indicates which industries are more likely to witness an increase in FDI activity. Agencies in developing and transition economies consider the best targets in their countries to be in the agricultural and agribusiness industry, along with the transport and telecommunications, hotel and restaurant, construction, and extractive industries. Moreover, there is an increase in intra African flows. More than 70% of all African outward-bound food, beverages and tobacco FDI is intra continental, with 44% of the investment capital flows accounted for by projects comprising primary production. This trend is encouraging, because it may help reduce Africa's dependence on extra continental FDI to stimulate its economies (UNCTAD, 2015). Greater efforts from governments are needed to meet the Comprehensive Africa Agriculture Development Programme's (CAADP's) goal of investing 10% of national budgets in agriculture and to attract FDI in ways that complement and promote rather than "crowd out" domestic agri-food system actors (see Box 3.3).

Rural and market infrastructures need to be improved, with the aim of improving access to education, training, inputs, markets, technology (including ICT) and finance. What will attract young people is not only the profitability of agriculture but also the basic services and the amenities that local rural areas and small towns can provide (IFAD, 2014b), hence the importance of investments in rural infrastructure such as roads, storage and market facilities, access to land, energy, cell phone coverage, water and technologies, and social protection schemes.

Finally, for agriculture to really become a competitive industry in developing countries, more investment in agricultural research is needed. Investing in agricultural research and development can help maintain a competitive edge. The "green revolution" – a combination of genetics and the heavy use of fertilisers and pesticides in the 1950s and 1960s – had an enormous impact on production, but also brought about a raft of ecological and health problems. Feeding the growing population of today and tomorrow cannot be sustained by this form of intensive, fuel- and chemical-dependent agriculture. As such, plant biotechnology could be a major tool in the fight against hunger and poverty, especially in developing countries. Biotechnology is a technique that uses living organisms to make or modify a product and improve plants or animals. Promising results have been reported through a range of biotechnology applications in improving plant breeding and controlling plant diseases. Diversity of the genetic base of the new plants, the reduction of chemical inputs, and the integration of soil, nutrient and water management on farms, are the three pillars of any new sustainable agriculture intensification effort (De Gannes and Borroto, 2016). If agriculture is going to assist in the development of sustainable rural livelihoods in developing countries, then policies focusing on improving technology use in this sector while ensuring environmental sustainability will need to be explored.

Greening and diversifying rural economies

The ILO defines green jobs as jobs that are attractive and generate good returns and income, and that reduce consumption of energy, raw materials and natural resources, reduce emissions of greenhouse gases, minimise the production of waste and pollution, protect and restore ecosystems and biodiversity, and help adapt to climate change. Examples of such jobs are those related to reforestation, land and water management, organic agriculture, the development of clean sources of energy, ecotourism, and recycling of agricultural waste.

Rural populations often depend directly on the environment and natural resources for their livelihoods, such as in agriculture, forestry, fisheries, mining and tourism. However, the ecosystem on which they rely is increasingly threatened by excessive and unsustainable exploitation. Greening the rural economy is key to boosting resource and labour productivity, reducing poverty, increasing income opportunities and improving youth well-being in rural areas (ILO, n.d.). The modernisation of agriculture and the expansion of ICT and products and services around renewable energies (e.g. solar, biogas) therefore hold employment opportunities for youth, especially rural youth.

The job creation potential through the production and supply of clean energy systems is significant in rural economies, as the majority of the 1.5 billion people who do not have access to electricity live in rural areas. The sources of renewable energy, e.g. sun, wind, biomass or geothermal sources, are often widely available in rural areas. This means that jobs related to the construction, operation, maintenance and distribution of the new energy system can be created, and the access to energy in rural areas will open doors for other productive activities such as food processing and storage, and the transport of agricultural products. Many of these jobs can be attractive to youth, as they require advanced skills and offer relatively better income opportunities (ILO, n.d.).

Ecotourism has significant economic and employment potential for rural areas. According to the World Travel and Tourism Council, in 2016 tourism directly created over 108 million jobs (3.6% of total employment) and this is expected to rise by 2.2% per annum to 138 million jobs (4.0% of total employment) in 2027 (World Travel and Tourism Council, 2017). In 2016, the industry directly and indirectly supported a total of 292 million jobs (9.6% of total employment) and this is expected to rise by 2.5% per annum to 382 million jobs in 2027 (World Travel and Tourism Council, 2017). This means that 1 in 11 jobs will be related to tourism. These jobs can be highly attractive to youth, as the sector and related activities are viewed as "modern" and requiring advanced skills, while constituting a good source of income. The potential of the tourism industry to contribute to economic and social development has also been recognised in the Sustainable Development Goals (Goals 8, 12 and 14).

A number of studies and quantitative assessments show that a global transformation to a greener economy could generate 15 to 60 million additional jobs globally over the next two decades, and lift tens of millions of workers out of poverty, with important improvements in productivity and income levels for rural communities (ILO, 2012).

Rural non-farm activities are the source of about 40% to 70% of rural households' income in Africa, Asia and Latin America (ILO, 2015a). Non-farm activities can include agri-food processing industries, home-based cottage industries, handicrafts and services such as storage, transport, basic farm equipment repair services, retail trading, extension services, tourism, and recreational services, among others. The amount spent on food and drink products, for example, has been increasing year on year in all parts of the world, and the related industries are a major source of employment worldwide. Food and drink processing in 2005 accounted for 4% of world GDP and employed 22 million people. The agro-processing sector is by far the most significant component in the agri-food industry, covering post-harvest activities, packaged agricultural raw materials, processing of intermediate goods and fabrication of final products derived from agriculture. Within the agro-industrial sector, food processing and beverages are the most important sub-sector in terms of value added, accounting for more than 50% of the total formal agro-processing sector in low-income and low-middle-income countries, whereas rural industries account for only between 20% and 25% of rural non-farm employment (da Silva et al., 2009).

> **Box 3.4. Blue Economy and the potential for large-scale job creation**
>
> Blue Economy is an open-source movement bringing together case studies that aims for a reduction in consumption without diminishing the economy. It looks at bundled portfolios of innovations based on pragmatic solutions to redefine the competitive business models which are the hallmark of our current paradigm. It relies on natural processes and physics, and derives inspiration from the natural environment around us to learn how living organisms have evolved over millennia to meet their requirements. Blue Economy tries to modify these phenomena to suit the material needs of human beings by changing existing business models to strive for sustainable development. The idea is that instead of constantly dealing with the waste in an environmentally harmful manner, residue of production becomes an input in another totally unrelated business to realise new and greater cash flows overall. The solutions it finds are determined by the local environment and physical/ecological characteristics.
>
> The example of mushroom cultivation best exemplifies Blue Economy and provides insight into future avenues for large-scale employment generation in developing countries. Mushrooms overtook coffee as the second most traded commodity in the 21st century, and their cultivation is labour intensive. Europe is the world's biggest market for mushrooms, and demand has been rising in North America as well. Mushrooms are traditionally farmed on agricultural waste, which is considered a nuisance and is often burned. Mushrooms convert plant waste into fruiting bodies, and it is these fruiting bodies which are consumed as edibles. Increasing demand for mushrooms presents the opportunity to utilise this waste-to-food chain to create thousands or even millions of jobs.
>
> But Blue Economy does not end here. There is potential to grow mushrooms on coffee waste. In the period between the coffee beans leaving the farm and ending up in brewing pots, 99.8% are discarded as waste and only 0.2% are ingested. Given that the annual world consumption of coffee in 2008 was 134 million bags, the total biomass wasted was 23.5 million tonnes. This biomass represents a perfect medium for growing mushrooms. The economic opportunities also make sense from a business point of view, since it involves a venture that converts waste into a nutritious yet cheap source of food, thus providing an economic stimulus for job creation in rural areas. With a minimum of two jobs being generated per coffee farm for mushroom cultivation, there are a total of 51.2 million jobs available worldwide in this venture. Entitled the Pulp-to-Protein model, it has been tried and tested in Colombia by Cenicafé, the Colombian Coffee Growers Federation research institute. By scientifically converting coffee biomass into food, it has helped achieve direct and indirect employment for 10 000 people, along with ensuring food security. Many other ventures are also involved in this approach and are reaping the benefits from a sustainable approach to mushroom cultivation.
>
> *Source:* Pauli, G. (2010), *The Blue Economy: 10 Years, 100 Innovations, 100 Million Jobs: Report to the Club of Rome.*

The share of employment in the services and manufacturing sectors (including agribusiness and agricultural services) is particularly important in South Asia. However, according to the ILO, on average 60% of the workers in the food and beverage industry are in the informal economy, often occupying precarious jobs. Non-farm activities can also be precarious, poorly remunerated and hazardous. Indeed, youth may be moving out of vulnerable work in agriculture into vulnerable work in the services industry. Those in rural areas especially tend to work as self-employed and casual wage labourers (ILO, 2015a). Many high-valued agri-food and non-food value chains are characterised by increasing levels of female participation (e.g. in Kenya, over 65% of workers in horticulture packhouses and farms are women) (da Silva et al., 2009). Promoting decent work in non-farm activities requires skills development, including in business management, technical skills, occupational safety and health, among others.

> **Box 3.5. Organic farming in Asia and the Pacific**
>
> Youth unemployment is a growing socio-economic challenge in Asia and the Pacific region, having increased by almost 5% between 2011 and 2013 to a rate of 11.3%, representing 33 million unemployed youth. In seeking productive employment opportunities and decent work, migration, either from rural to urban areas or outward to another country, is a popular choice among youth (UNESCAP, 2016). Young people with a certain amount of schooling do not see a future in pursuing a farming career. Often, they also do not possess the knowledge of their parents and grandparents. They are attracted to towns and cities by the prospects of taking on more prestigious employment.
>
> The Asian Farmers' Association for Sustainable Rural Development confirms that the number of organic farms has increased in the region and that mostly youth are involved in the promotion of organic farms (AFA, 2015a). For youth, organic farming provides some meaning in their work, as well as more opportunities for innovation and learning from old and new ways of farming. The global market for organic products continues to grow. The recent International Foundation for Organic Agriculture (IFOAM) report *The World of Organic Agriculture: Statistics and Emerging Trends 2016* estimates that Asia has the third-largest market for organic products. Forty percent of the world's organic producers are in Asia, followed by Africa (26%), and many countries in Asia are encouraging organic agriculture. While the focus has been on exports, there is also the potential for growth in domestic markets.
>
> In Sri Lanka, the domestic market for organic products is expanding from urban communities to rural areas, where local communities are increasing their consumption of organic foods. In Viet Nam, domestic demand for organic products, particularly tea and vegetables, is growing. Building on the recognition that the market for organic products is expanding and organic farming is attracting youth, a series of initiatives focusing on skills development for youth to seize opportunities in the organic food market are being implemented in the Asia Pacific region.
>
> Bhutan has committed to a 100% organic target, and organic farming is now seen as an attractive and better way of farming, with high school and college graduates choosing organic farming as a livelihood and a business opportunity (Willer and Lernoud, 2016). The Bhutanese initiative Organic Farmers Exchange Programme aims to reduce youth unemployment by promoting organic farming as a meaningful profession. The programme offers study tours and targets young villagers who will dedicate their lives to organic farming and village life. The intention is to facilitate integrated small-scale quality exchange by offering young, preferably female, Bhutanese farmers the chance to experience organic farming in Austria within a particular socio cultural context. Similarly, the Austrian farmers will be visiting the organic farms of their Bhutanese colleagues in order to understand the particularities of Bhutanese farming. The aim will

> be to establish a long-term connection and exchange at the farmers' level to mutually benefit and strengthen the organic grassroots movement – highlighting differences as well as similarities. This will stimulate a growing awareness among young farmers that organic multi-resource farming is not an outdated activity.
>
> ActionAid Thailand works with the Sustainable Agricultural Foundation and networks to promote organic farming. The project "Building Capacity and Expanding the Group of New Generation Farmers in the Methods of Sustainable Agriculture" supports young farmers' capacity building on effective farming technology, such as local seed breeding and sharing experiences to replicate best practices and lessons learned among youth. It aims to develop and raise the level of a cadre of new-generation farmers to serve as peer leaders. The first phase of the project (2013-14) included the implementation of a training curriculum. The training included principles of sustainable farming; expansion of the farmers' network through self-empowerment; primary collection and preservation of indigenous seeds and plants; analysis and development of markets for produce; distillation of the lessons learned from the sustainable farming plots; participation in lessons learned forums with others working in this area domestically and internationally (e.g. Viet Nam); and production of educational media in various formats. During this phase, five new-generation farmers were trained as peer leaders in organic agriculture in the Sanam Chai Khet district.

Ensuring social and environmental safeguards

Since the early 2000s, large-scale industrial agriculture has been promoted in tropical countries in response to the global increased demand for food, fibre and fuel (Biénabe et al., 2016). This has led to deforestation and the use of chemicals to increase productivity, to the detriment of biodiversity and the environment. Rising concerns over these issues and denunciations have forced multinational agri-food companies to ensure that they themselves and actors along their supply chain are applying responsible and sustainable methods of production and manufacturing. Multinational companies play an important role in ensuring inclusive value chains and also in training and hiring young people. Several guidelines and principles to ensure responsible business conducts exist, but these are not always applied.

The UN Global Compact is a framework with 11 principles covering the areas of human rights, labour, the environment and anti-corruption. By adhering to these principles, companies commit to a different approach to doing business and can make a positive impact on food systems and sustainable agriculture. As part of its decent work principle, the UN Global Compact community calls on businesses to promote entrepreneurship among young people and invest in youth-owned enterprises (e.g. by integrating them into their supply chains or providing venture capital to new enterprises). In 2014, the UN Global Compact launched the Food and Agriculture Business (FAB) Principles, the first set of six global voluntary business principles for the entire food and agricultural sector. One of the principles relates to the creation of decent work. UN Global Compact companies are invited to report on progress against the FAB Principles, but are not required to sign on to them.

FAO developed the first handbook on sustainable food value chain development, *Developing Sustainable Food Value Chains: Guiding Principles* (Neven, 2014), which provides practical guidance and shares innovative solutions emerging from the field. The handbook describes how to tackle value chain constraints one by one and how value chains create added value and growth loops (an investment loop, a multiplier loop and a progress loop), including by creating decent employment. The handbook suggests that as productivity of farm labour increases, opportunities for job growth will happen mainly in service provision further downstream in the food value chain (e.g. processing, trade) and in non-food value chains. As an example, the handbook mentions Blue Skies, a European fruit processing company which has operations in Ghana. The company invested in a processing and packaging plant which employs 1 500 staff, with around 60% permanent positions, and 40% of the management team is women (including the General Manager). The company pays almost four times the minimum wage and ensures a safe working environment for employees. Around 200 commercially oriented small-scale farmers and a few large plantation operations supply the produce. Blue Skies provides free training, free technical support and interest-free loans for inputs and equipment to small-scale farmers (Neven, 2014).

Youth-specific guidelines are starting to emerge, such as the Netherlands Development Organisation and the Royal Tropical Institute's (KIT's) principles to address youth- and gender-inclusive agri-food chains (Pyburn et al., 2015). In 2014, the Committee on World Food Security developed the *Principles for Responsible Investment in Agriculture and Food Systems*, in which Principle 4 is to engage and empower youth (OECD/FAO, 2015). In 2015, the OECD and FAO developed guidance to help enterprises observe standards of responsible business conduct to ensure that their operations do not lead to adverse impacts, but contribute to sustainable development. This guidance integrates the dimensions of child labour and youth employment: "Provide appropriate training, education and mentorship programmes for youth to increase their capacity and/or access to decent work and entrepreneurship, and promote access to training by women" (OECD/FAO, 2016).

Raising the voices of rural youth in policy dialogue

While many countries have renewed their commitment to support youth employment, the role of agriculture in employment for young people has not yet been translated into public policies (AGRA, 2015). The integration of youth in agricultural sector policies remains a challenge. *The State of Youth Policy in 2014*, produced by the Youth Policy Press, indicated that despite advances in most countries, a number of challenges remain, including funding, as well as legal and institutional frameworks (AGRA, 2015).

Participation of young women and men in the design and implementation of policies is an important part of ensuring that their needs and aspirations are taken into account. Little information is available on the level of participation of youth in policy processes related to agriculture and rural development, especially at national level. But in 2012, the United Nations Inter-Agency Network on Youth Development, through a survey of the 13 000 respondents representing 186 countries from all regions around the world, found that young people, especially those from rural areas, have limited opportunities for effective participation in decision making processes (AGRA, 2015).

The first barrier is that youth may be perceived as having little capacity to shape their own destinies (AGRA, 2015), and in certain cases are not allowed to speak out or voice their concerns. It is even more challenging for women who face traditional norms excluding them from any decision making process. When looking at youth participation in policies, different dimensions need to be considered: who represents youth, how they participate and in which processes they participate. For agricultural policies to be more conducive to youth, youth representation needs to match the diversity of this group, as they may require different sets of interventions to facilitate their engagement in different segments of the agriculture value chains.

There are different levels of participation; the UN Youth programme (MIJARC/IFAD/FAO, 2012) identified five: providing information, consulting (decision maker initiated), consulting (youth-initiated), shared decision making or co-management, and autonomy. There is still a long way to go to reach the shared decision making and autonomy end of the continuum. Rural youth need to acquire certain skills, e.g. communication and leadership, in order to feel more confident and participate actively in policy dialogues. They also need to be supported in order to better understand existing policies, so that they are able to provide inputs that will make those policies more responsive to their needs. These skills are also important within youth groups/organisations to build trust and a common voice, as well as when partnering with other organisations.

By organising themselves in youth-only organisations or joining existing mixed organisations or networks, youth can find sustainable channels to get their voices heard at the local and national levels. However, there are still a small number of organisations representing only rural youth, and they often lack resources and bargaining power. But some examples can be inspiring.

This is the case of the network of young producers and agricultural professionals of Togo (REJEPPAT), created as a youth college within a national producers' organisation. Beyond its participation in drafting national policy on access to land for youth and women, REJEPPAT's lobby resulted in the state clearing farmland and supporting rural youth setting up in farming. When supporting these organisations (youth-only or mixed), special measures need to be taken to build the capacity of rural youth groups and to facilitate young women's participation, e.g. setting quotas in membership and raising awareness among men (FAO/CTA/IFAD, 2014).

In Cambodia, the Farmer and Nature Net has established a youth committee, which is represented on its board. The young farmers are also being developed into young leaders and farmer entrepreneurs (AFA, 2015a). In the Philippines, the Asian Farmers' Association for Sustainable Rural Development is pushing for the crafting of a Magna Carta of Young Farmers that will recognise the aspirations of young women and men farmers and promote their roles and contributions to family farming. The proposed bill will protect the rights of young farmers aged 15-40 years; establish programmes for young farmers, e.g. agriculture-sensitive educational curriculum and broader scholarships for all agriculture-related courses; promote "farm take-over" schemes; and institutionalise young farmers' representation in all agricultural policy-making bodies and other agencies with reserved seats for youth (AFA, 2015b).

An initial step from the government side to include youth in agricultural policy dialogue is to make the participation of different youth groups systematic in consultations (and provide resources to support this participation) giving them space to examine existing policies and evaluate alternatives. Ultimately, youth are the best experts when it comes to expressing the challenges they face, deciding on their priorities for the future and designing solutions. Co-ordination between different ministries (youth, agriculture, labour, trade, social protection, etc.) should also be enhanced to support integrated and co-ordinated approaches that facilitate youth's engagement in the agriculture and agri-food sectors, and support decent work. Too often, sectoral and youth ministries act independently on issues that affect youth, thereby affecting the identification and allocation of sources of funding targeting youth and governments' capacity to monitor and evaluate the impact of their interventions (Youth Policy Press; AGRA, 2015). Concerted national dialogues and efforts should also include non-governmental organisations (NGOs), development partners and the private sector, especially when targeting special value chains.

The Global Initiative on Decent Jobs for Youth was launched in February 2016 in New York, under the auspices of the United Nations Economic and Social Council (ECOSOC) Youth Forum 2016, with more than 20 ministers of youth and over 500 youth delegates in attendance. The objective of the Initiative is to facilitate an extensive partnership with governments, businesses and youth organisations, with a view to promoting new employment opportunities and helping young people acquire the appropriate skills. The Initiative includes a focus on promoting decent employment opportunities for young people in agriculture and in the rural economy. While agriculture cannot be the only answer to youth employment, for those who decide to engage in the broader agricultural sector, this focus on rural economies, if followed by appropriate financial and political actions, can provide concrete answers for rural youth.

Providing skills development and second-chance programmes for rural youth

Large skills gaps go hand in hand with low-productivity employment opportunities and act as a major impediment in economic development. Despite high unemployment and underemployment rates in many developing countries, private sector employers struggle to find qualified candidates to fill posts, even in promising sectors where labour demand is high. At the same time, the large number of low-educated and low-skilled employees, particularly in the informal sector, widens the productivity gap. In sub-Saharan Africa, 58% of 15-17 year-olds have already left school and in North Africa this figure is 25%. Traditional technical and vocational education and training (TVET) programmes either fail to reach out-of-school and low educated youth or do not provide training in subjects that are relevant for the labour market. The average vocational training enrolment rate by secondary school students in Africa is only 10% and only between 2% and 6% of educational budgets are earmarked for TVET.

Despite the potential for new jobs in agri-food value chains and non-farm activities in rural areas, the majority of rural youth in developing countries are low educated and low skilled. Skills mismatch, mostly related to underqualification, hinders attempts at moving up the value chain or getting better jobs. Various training modalities exist (Table 3.1) and while there are plenty of evaluations and analysis on traditional TVET programmes, not much is known about the role of the private sector, especially small and medium enterprises and informal businesses, in youth skills development.

Table 3.1. Training modalities in developing countries

Training modalities	Strengths	Weaknesses
Public training centres	- have a capacity to deliver courses in capital-intensive trades - follow-up national policies and may address priority skills needs, support national economic and social development	- often inflexible and irresponsive to market demand; routinely deliver the same courses without regard to demand - tend to deliver courses with outdated curricula - commonly underfunded, with serious impact felt on quality and access - overly centralised training systems leave institutions little freedom for flexibility and initiative - unable to offer broad access to training, due to limited seating capacity and financial constraints - do not reach low-skilled and out-of-school youth
NGOs	- important providers of training in many African countries - commonly provide training for vulnerable groups free of charge or for low fees - high proportion of women in training - better managed and more responsive to labour market needs and graduate employability	- show large variation in quality - tend to focus on training requiring low capital investment - often fragmented and not part of a coherent skills strategy
Private training providers	- fastest growing segment of training provision - able to absorb the growing demand for technical education and skills training flexibly	- the range of programmes and quality of delivery vary and may be rather low - high tuition fees tend to exclude the poorest segments of the population - more operationally flexible and less responsive to the market demand for skills
Traditional apprenticeship	- major training avenue in the informal economy - based on on-the-job instruction and show high relevance to actual job requirement in the informal economy - offer training opportunities to the poorest and least educated segments of the population - self-financed and self-regulated - in general, very effective and large coverage among out-of-school youth	- training is often of poor quality and generally does not integrate technical innovations - requires long periods for acquiring a trade - skills acquired are often limited to the demands of the informal economy and may be unsuitable to the needs of modern industry - there are acute problems of signalling acquired skills to potential employers, since most training is carried out in the informal sector and is not recognised
Enterprise-based training	- self-financed and self-regulated - based on actual tasks performed by workers - closely linked to existing production technology	- mostly provided by large firms, where it targets highly skilled positions and workers with highest level of education - small participation of small and medium enterprises (SMEs) - do not reach low-skilled and out-of-school youth

Source: Adapted from AfDB/OECD (2008).

SMEs offer great potential for youth skills development. In Africa, SMEs create the majority of jobs (AfDB/OECD/UNDP, 2017). As such, the potential for these actors to train young people and hire them is tremendous. However, SMEs are reluctant to invest in training youth because the costs are immediate but the benefits only accrue over time; moreover, the risk of trained workers being poached by other firms is high (DEG/BCG, 2016). Thus far, private sector participation in training remains largely limited to multinational and large domestic firms (Table 3.2). Evidence suggests that employers' direct involvement in training is an effective way to equip young people with soft and hard skills needed to close the skills gap (Glick, Huang and Mejia, 2015.). Little information exists on incentives that work for SMEs to contribute to youth skills development, as few of them participate in training, and also because many operate in the informal sector. More incentive schemes to involve SMEs in rural youth skills development should be provided.

Policies and public and private investment can be designed to intentionally support SMEs and local value chains that create decent youth employment. Policies and programmes can support the strengthening of smallholders and small and medium agribusinesses and create specific incentives for youth, for example by supporting and legally empowering youth co-operatives and youth participation in mixed co-operatives, and providing financial and/or technical support to businesses that hire young people. Employment services should also support motivated young entrepreneurs in rural areas to develop new value-added products and services along the agri-food value chain. Access to finance and social protection will be crucial to enable rural youth to become entrepreneurs and develop SMEs.

Table 3.2. Constraints and incentives for private sector engagement in TVET programmes

Firm size (formal or informal)	Type of training provided	Desired level of education of candidates	Level of firms' engagement in TVET	Incentives for firms	Constraints for firms
Multinationals (formal)	Skills training Entrepreneurship promotion	Higher education Secondary education	High to medium	Corporate social responsibility; direct productivity or commercial benefits (i.e. to have a better skilled workforce or more reliable supply and distribution networks for their in-country operations) Tax rebates	Finding qualified candidates
Domestic firms (formal)	Skills training (manufacturing and services) Job placement	Higher education Secondary education	Medium	Skilled workforce Tax rebates	Finding qualified candidates High cost High turnover rate
Domestic SMEs (informal)		Secondary education	Low	Skilled workforce Subsidies/vouchers to upgrade and formalise apprenticeship systems Collective training in order to lower costs	High costs relative to benefits Lack of information Lack of technical and administrative resources High turnover and risk of trained workers being poached by other firms
Micro firms (informal)		Low	Low	Receiving training themselves	Collective engagement in organising and financing interventions is difficult, due to diversity and large number of micro firms. Fear of competition by more qualified apprentices

Source: Authors' own elaboration.

> **Box 3.6. Developing entrepreneurial culture and skills: UNIDO's Entrepreneurship Curriculum Programme**
>
> UNIDO's Entrepreneurship Curriculum Programme (ECP) is a cost-effective investment in the development of entrepreneurial capacity of young people. ECP is inclusive since it reaches out to both girls and boys in rural and urban areas.
>
> Entrepreneurship is introduced as a subject in general secondary schools or technical and vocational schools on a nationwide basis. Universities and colleges serve as centres of excellence to support national efforts to promote entrepreneurship and technology absorbing capacities. Young people acquire personal qualities such as self-confidence, innovation and creativity, the ability to take initiatives, as well as the willingness to take calculated risks and to collaborate. They learn to save, invest and grow. These competencies help them select and shape their career path as employees or entrepreneurs.
>
> The curriculum is action-oriented: more than 50% of the programme's time consists of practical research in identifying business opportunities, assessing resources for setting up and steering a business, and learning from successful entrepreneurs in their companies and in the classroom.
>
> UNIDO assists authorities in developing their own curriculum with syllabus, teachers' guides, textbooks, monitoring and evaluation tools, assessment guidelines, training ECP teachers, piloting and ultimately embarking on a nationwide roll-out of an entrepreneurship curriculum with the initiatives of the national authorities.
>
> Several countries are currently implementing ECP, and more are preparing for it. With its expertise and international knowledge network, UNIDO supports the development of each country's own ECP. An important factor for success is the building of partnerships with the local private sector.
>
> UNIDO also supports the efforts of national authorities in improving the performance of public services to encourage entrepreneurs to start and operate businesses. The goal is to create an environment conducive for an entrepreneurial society where initiatives by existing and potential entrepreneurs can unfold, and lay the ground for private sector development.
>
> *Source:* ECP website, https://www.unido.org/our-focus/creating-shared-prosperity/agribusiness-and-rural-entrepreneurship-development/entrepreneurship-curriculum-programme.

Notes

[1] http://reports.weforum.org/enabling-trade-from-valuation-to-action/enabling-trade-from-farm-to-fork/a6-case-studies-f2f/nigerian-cassava-flour-broadening-value-chains-for-traditional-crops/.

[2] http://www.fao.org/rural-employment/resources/detail/en/c/389287/.

References

AFA (2015a), "A viable future: Attracting the youth to agriculture", *Issue Paper Volume 7*, No. 1, Asian Farmers' Association for Sustainable Rural Development, Quezon City, Philippines, http://asianfarmers.org/wp-content/uploads/2015/07/AFA-Issue-Paper_-for-web.pdf.

AFA (2015b), "A magna carta of young farmers: Promoting the contributions of young women and men farmers to family farming", *Policy Brief 5*, Asian Farmers' Association for Sustainable Rural Development, Quezon City, Philippines, http://asianfarmers.org/wp-content/uploads/2015/02/5-Young-Farmers.pdf.

AfDB/OECD (2008), *African Economic Outlook 2007/2008*, OECD Publishing, Paris, http://dx.doi.org/10.1787/aeo-2008-en.

AfDB/OECD/UNDP (2017), *African Economic Outlook 2017: Entrepreneurship and Industrialisation*, OECD Publishing, Paris, http://dx.doi.org/10.1787/aeo-2017-en.

AfDB/OECD/UNDP (2016), *African Economic Outlook 2016: Sustainable Cities and Structural Transformation*, OECD Publishing, Paris, http://dx.doi.org/10.1787/aeo-2016-en.

AfDB/OECD/UNDP (2015), African Economic Outlook 2015: Regional Development and Spatial Inclusion, OECD Publishing, Paris, http://dx.doi.org/10.1787/aeo-2015-en.

AfDB/OECD/UNDP (2014), *African Economic Outlook 2014: Global Value Chains and Africa's Industrialisation*, OECD Publishing, Paris, http://dx.doi.org/10.1787/aeo-2014-en.

AfDB et al. (2012), *African Economic Outlook 2012: Promoting Youth Employment*, OECD Publishing, Paris, http://dx.doi.org/10.1787/aeo-2012-en.

AGRA (2015), "Africa agriculture status report 2015: Youth in agriculture in sub-Saharan Africa, *Issue No. 3*, Alliance for a Green Revolution in Africa, Nairobi, Kenya.

Allen, T. and P. Heinrigs (2016), "Emerging opportunities in the West African food economy", *West African Papers*, No. 1, OECD Publishing, Paris, http://dx.doi.org/10.1787/5jlvfj4968jb-en.

Arias, P. et al. (2013), *Smallholder Integration in Changing Food Markets*, Food and Agriculture Organization of the United Nations, Rome.

Aulakh, J. and A. Regmi (2013), "Post-harvest food losses estimation - Development of consistent methodology", Food and Agriculture Organization website, http://www.fao.org/fileadmin/templates/ess/documents/meetings_and_workshops/GS_SAC_2013/Improving_methods_for_estimating_post_harvest_losses/Final_PHLs_Estimation_6-13-13.pdf (accessed December 2017).

Barlow, S. (2011), "The Enter-Growth project – Sri Lanka: Applying a market development lens to an ILO local enterprise development project", *Employment Report No. 11*, International Labour Office, Small Enterprise Programme, Job Creation and Enterprise Development Department, Geneva.

Bennell, P. (2007), "Promoting livelihood opportunities for rural youth", *Knowledge and Skills for Development Paper*, International Fund for Agricultural Development, Rome.

Biénabe, E. et al. (2016), "Introduction", in *Développement durable et filières tropicales*, Centre de coopération internationale en recherche agronomique pour le développement and Agence Française de Développement, Editions Quae, Paris.

Bolwig, S. et al. (2010), "Integrating poverty and environmental concerns into value-chain analysis: A conceptual framework", *Development Policy Review*, Vol. 28/2, Blackwell Publishing, Oxford, pp. 173 194.

Chandra, A.C. and L.A. Lontoh (2010), "Regional food security and trade policy in Southeast Asia: The role of ASEAN", *Series on Trade and Food Security – Policy Report 3*, International Institute for Sustainable Development, Winnipeg, MB.

Christiaensen, L. and G. Lawin (2017), "Maximizing agriculture's contribution to the jobs agenda", in *Côte d'Ivoire Jobs Diagnostic—Employment, Productivity, and Inclusion for Poverty Reduction*, World Bank, Washington, DC.

da Silva, C.A. et al. (eds.) (2009), *Agro-industries for Development*, Food and Agriculture Organization of the United Nations and United Nations Industrial Development Organization by arrangement with CAB International, Rome.

DEG/BCG (2016), *Bridging the Skills Gaps in Developing Countries: A Practical Guide for Private-Sector Companies*, prepared by DEG – Deutsche Investitions- und Entwicklungsgesellschaft and The Boston Consulting Group for the Association of European Development Finance Institutions within the Let's Work Partnership, Cologne and Brussels.

De Gannes, V. and C. Borroto (2016), *Agricultural Development and Food Security in Developing Nations*, edited by W. Ganpat, R. Dyer and W A. Isaac, IGI Global, Hershey, PA.

Duteurtre, G. et al. (2016), "Les alliances entre acteurs des filières pour un développement durable des territoires au Vietnam", in *Développement durable et filières tropicales*, Centre de coopération internationale en recherche agronomique pour le développement and Agence Française de Développement, Editions Quae, Paris.

FAO (2016), *The State of World Fisheries and Aquaculture 2016: Contributing to Food Security and Nutrition for All*, Food and Agriculture Organization of the United Nations, Rome.

FAO (2014), *Youth and Aquaculture in Africa* (infographic), Food and Agriculture Organization of the United Nations, Rome, http://www.fao.org/assets/infographics/FAO-Infographic-Youth-Aquaculture-Africa-en.pdf.

FAO (2013), *Trends and Impacts of Foreign Investment in Developing Country Agriculture: Evidence from Case Studies*, Food and Agriculture Organization of the United Nations, Rome.

FAO/CTA/IFAD (2014), *Youth and Agriculture: Key Challenges and Concrete Solutions*, Food and Agriculture Organization of the United Nations, Rome.

Glick, P., C. Huang and N. Mejia (2015), *The Private Sector and Youth Skills and Employment Programs in Low- and Middle-Income Countries*, World Bank Group, Washington, DC.

Hathie, I. (25 July 2016), "Comment l'agriculture peut-elle répondre à l'arrivée massive de jeunes Sénégalais sur le marché du travail?", Fondation FARM Blog, http://www.fondation-farm.org/zoe.php?s=blogfarm&w=wt&idt=3048.

HELVETAS Swiss Intercooperation (2013), "Food Security, Food Sovereignty", *Position paper*, HELVETAS Swiss Intercooperation, Zurich.

Henderson, J.R. and K.T. McNamara (2000), "The location of food manufacturing plant investments in corn belt counties", *Journal of Agricultural and Resource Economics*, Vol. 25/2, Western Agricultural Economics Association, Milwaukee, WI, pp. 680 697.

IFAD (2014a), "Sustainable inclusion of smallholders in agricultural value chains", *Commodity Value Chain Development Projects*, International Fund for Agricultural Development, Rome.

IFAD (2014b), "Supporting rural young people in IFAD projects", *Lessons Learned*, International Fund for Agricultural Development, Rome.

ILO (n.d.), *Greening the Rural Economy and Green Jobs*, Decent Work in the Rural Economy, Policy Guidance Notes, International Labour Office, Geneva.

ILO (2015a), *Global Employment Trends for Youth 2015: Scaling Up Investments in Decent Jobs for Youth*, International Labour Office, Geneva.

ILO (2015b), *Value Chain Development for Decent Work: How to Create Employment and Improve Working Conditions in Targeted Sectors*, Second Edition, International Labour Office, Geneva.

ILO (2012), *Working Towards Sustainable Development: Opportunities for Decent Work and Social Inclusion in a Green Economy*, International Labour Office, Geneva.

Kew, J. (2015), *Africa's Young Entrepreneurs: Unlocking the Potential for a Brighter Future*, Development Unit for New Enterprise, University of Cape Town, Rondebosch, South Africa.

Lowder, S., B. Carisma and J. Skoet (2012), "Who invests in agriculture and how much? An empirical review of the relative size of various investments in agriculture in low- and middle-income countries", *ESA Working Paper No. 12-09*, Agricultural Development Economics Division, Food and Agriculture Organization of the United Nations, Rome.

MIJARC/IFAD/FAO (2012), "Summary of the findings of the project implemented by MIJARC in collaboration with FAO and IFAD: 'Facilitating access of rural youth to agricultural activities'", The Farmers' Forum Youth Session, 18 February 2012, Rome.

NEPAD (2013), *Agriculture in Africa: Transformation and Outlook*, New Partnership for African Development, Johannesburg, South Africa.

Neven, D. (2014), *Developing Sustainable Food Value Chains: Guiding Principles*, Food and Agriculture Organization of the United Nations, Rome.

OECD (n.d.), "Trends in aid to agriculture and rural development (ARD)", OECD Statistics, http://www.oecd.org/dac/stats/Trends%20in%20aid%20to%20Agriculture%20and%20Rural%20Development.pdf.

OECD (2016), *A New Rural Development Paradigm for the 21st Century: A Toolkit for Developing Countries*, Development Centre Studies, OECD Publishing, Paris, http://dx.doi.org/10.1787/9789264252271-en.

OECD (2015), "Aid to agriculture and rural development", OECD Development Assistance Committee, https://www.oecd.org/dac/stats/documentupload/Aid%20to%20agriculture%20and%20rural%20development%20data.pdf.

OECD/FAO (2016), *OECD-FAO Guidance for Responsible Agricultural Supply Chains*, OECD Publishing, Paris, http://dx.doi.org/10.1787/9789264251052-en.

OECD/FAO (2015), *OECD-FAO Agricultural Outlook 2015*, OECD Publishing, Paris, http://dx.doi.org/10.1787/agr_outlook-2015-en.

Pauli, G. (2010), *The Blue Economy: 10 Years, 100 Innovations, 100 Million Jobs: Report to the Club of Rome*, Paradigm Publications, Taos, NM.

Pyburn, R. et al. (2015), "Unleashing potential: Gender and youth inclusive agri-food chains", *KIT Working Papers*, 2015-7, Royal Tropical Institute and SNV, Amsterdam.

Schaffnit Chatterjee, C. (2014), "Agricultural value chains in Sub-Saharan Africa: From a development challenge to a business opportunity", *Current Issues Emerging Markets*, Deutsche Bank Research, Frankfurt.

Signé, L. (16 October 2017), "The quest for food security and agricultural transformation in Africa: Is the CAADP the answer?", Brookings Africa in Focus Blog, https://www.brookings.edu/blog/africa-in-focus/2017/10/16/the-quest-for-food-security-and-agricultural-transformation-in-africa-is-the-caadp-the-answer/.

Staatz, J. and F. Hollinger (2016), "West African food systems and changing consumer demands", *West African Papers*, No. 4, OECD Publishing, Paris, http://dx.doi.org/10.1787/b165522b-en.

UNCTAD (2015), *World Investment Report: Reforming International Investment Governance*, United Nations Conference on Trade and Development, Geneva.

UNESCAP (2016), *Economic and Social Survey of Asia and the Pacific 2015: Year-End Update*, United Nations Economic and Social Commission for Asia and the Pacific, Bangkok.

UNIDROIT/FAO/IFAD (2015), *Legal Guide on Contract Farming*, International Institute for the Unification of Private Law, Food and Agriculture Organization of the United Nations and International Fund for Agricultural Development, Rome.

Willer, H. and J. Lernoud (eds.) (2016), *The World of Organic Agriculture: Statistics and Emerging Trends 2016*, Research Institute of Organic Agriculture, Frick, and IFOAM – Organics International, Bonn.

WIPO (2017), *Geographical Indications: An Introduction*, World Intellectual Property Organization, Geneva, http://www.wipo.int/edocs/pubdocs/en/geographical/952/wipo_pub_952.pdf.

World Bank/IFAD (2017), "Rural youth employment", paper commissioned by the German Federal Ministry for Economic Cooperation and Development as an Input Document for the G20 - Development Working Group.

World Travel and Tourism Council (2017), *Travel and Tourism Economic Impact 2017*, World Travel and Tourism Council, London.

ORGANISATION FOR ECONOMIC CO-OPERATION AND DEVELOPMENT

The OECD is a unique forum where governments work together to address the economic, social and environmental challenges of globalisation. The OECD is also at the forefront of efforts to understand and to help governments respond to new developments and concerns, such as corporate governance, the information economy and the challenges of an ageing population. The Organisation provides a setting where governments can compare policy experiences, seek answers to common problems, identify good practice and work to co-ordinate domestic and international policies.

The OECD member countries are: Australia, Austria, Belgium, Canada, Chile, the Czech Republic, Denmark, Estonia, Finland, France, Germany, Greece, Hungary, Iceland, Ireland, Israel, Italy, Japan, Korea, Latvia, Luxembourg, Mexico, the Netherlands, New Zealand, Norway, Poland, Portugal, the Slovak Republic, Slovenia, Spain, Sweden, Switzerland, Turkey, the United Kingdom and the United States. The European Union takes part in the work of the OECD.

OECD Publishing disseminates widely the results of the Organisation's statistics gathering and research on economic, social and environmental issues, as well as the conventions, guidelines and standards agreed by its members.

OECD DEVELOPMENT CENTRE

The OECD Development Centre was established in 1962 as an independent platform for knowledge sharing and policy dialogue between OECD member countries and developing economies, allowing these countries to interact on an equal footing. Today, 27 OECD countries and 25 non-OECD countries are members of the Centre. The Centre draws attention to emerging systemic issues likely to have an impact on global development and more specific development challenges faced by today's developing and emerging economies. It uses evidence-based analysis and strategic partnerships to help countries formulate innovative policy solutions to the global challenges of development.

For more information on the Centre and its members, please see *www.oecd.org/dev*.

www.ingramcontent.com/pod-product-compliance
Lightning Source LLC
Chambersburg PA
CBHW082347220526
45470CB00008B/2681